CODING

Series 2

THIS BOOK INCLUDES :

"C++ for Beginners + Python Coding "

By Jason Clark

C++ FOR BEGINNERS

PYTHON CODING

C++

FOR BEGINNERS

The Ultimate Guide To Learn C++
Programming Step-by-Step
By Tom Clark

Introduction

C++ is a for the most part significant programming language proposed to make programming more charming for the authentic software engineer. With the exception of minor subtleties, C++ is a superset of the C programming language. In spite of the working environments given by C, C++ gives adaptable and fruitful work environments to depicting new sorts. A softwareengineer can disperse application into sensible pieces by depicting new sorts that enthusiastically match the musings of the application. This technique for program construction is routinely called information thought. Objects of some client depicted sorts contain type data. Such things can be utilized well and securely in settings in which their sortcan't be hinder mined at arrange time. Adventures utilizing objects of such sorts are constantly called object based. Right when utilized well, these situations accomplish more confined, more plainly obvious, and simpler to really focus on programs.

The significant idea in C++ is class. A class is a client depicted sort. Classes give up informationcovering, ensured instatement of information, seen sort change for client depicted sorts, dynamic shaping, client-controlled memory the heads, and instruments for over-upsetting chiefs. C++ gives much better work environments to type checking and for passing on separation than C does. It's like way contains upgrades that are not immediate identified with classes, including significant constants, inline substitution of cutoff points, default work clashes, over-inconvenience work names, free store the boss's administrators, and a reference type. C++ holds C's capacity to manage the central objects of the equipment (bits, bytes, words, addresses, and so on) This permits the client portrayed sorts to be executed with an awesome level of ability. C++ is an intermediate level language, as it contains a confirmation of both unquestionable level and low-level language features. C++ is a free form,statically type, multiparadigm, compiled general purpose language. C++ is an Object-Oriented Programming language at some points isn't totally Object Oriented. Its features like Friend and Virtual, contradict a bit of the essential OOPS features. Hence you can call it both an intermediate programming language as well as object-oriented programming language. C++ and its standard libraries are expected for portability. The current execution will run on most systems that help C. C libraries can be used from a C++ program, and most instruments that

Chapter 1

1.1 Description

C++, as we know in general is a wing to C language and was made by Bjarne Stroustrup at belllabs. C++ was intended to give Simula's working environments to program relationship close by C's ability and flexibility for structures programming. It was needed to give that to credibletasks inside a colossal section of a time of the thought.

The objective was really simple at thattime it didn't involve any sort of innovation and was quite a compromise on the flexibility andefficiency of the language. While an unassuming degree of progress emerged all through theextended length, efficiency and flexibility have been kept up without deal. While, the destinations for C++ have been refined, clarified, and made all the more express all through the long haul, C++ as used today clearly reflects its exceptional focuses. Most effort has been utilized on the early years because the arrangement decisions taken early chose the further improvement of the language. It is also less complex to keep an unquestionable perspective when one has had various years to see the aftereffects of decisions.

In this short book we will talk about how C++ language emerged over the time and what type of programming updates have occurred over the years.

Chapter 2

2.1 First Programming Language (Simula)

2.1.1 History

The essential object-oriented programming language was made during the 1960s at the Norwegian Registering Center in Oslo, by two Norwegian PC specialists—Ole-Johan Dahl (1931-2002) and Kristen Nygaard (1926-2002).

Kristen Nygaard, a MS in number juggling at the College of Oslo, started creating PC entertainment programs in 1957. He was searching for a better strategy than depict the heterogeneity and the movement of a system. To go further with his contemplations on an ordinary scripting language for depicting a system, Nygaard comprehended that he requiredsomeone with more PC programming capacities than he had, thusly he arrived at Ole-Johan Dahl, in like manner a MS in math and one of the Norway's chief PC analyst, who obliged himin January 1962.

In 1966 the English PC scientist Tony Hoare introduced record class create, which Dahl and Nygaard connected with prefixing and various features to meet their necessities for another summarized measure thought. The essential customary importance of Simula 67 appeared inMay 1967. In June 1967 a gathering was held to standardize the language and start differentexecutions. Dahl proposed to unite the sort and the class thought. This provoked real discussions, and the suggestion was excused by the board. SIMULA 67 was formally standardized on the chief fulfilling of the SIMULA Rules Gathering in February 1968.

Simula 6 contained huge quantities of the thoughts that are presently open in standard Object-oriented like Java, C++, and C#.

2.2 C++ Language evolution

The C++ programming language has a bunch of encounters getting back to 1979, when Bjarne Stroustrup was handling position for his Ph.D. Proposition. One of the vernaculars Stroustrup got the opportunity to work with was a language called Simula, which as the name recommends is a language essentially proposed for reenactments. The Simula 67 language - which was the variety that Stroustrup worked with - is seen as the vital language to help the article masterminded programming perspective. Stroustrup found that this perspective was outstandingly important for programming improvement, in any case the Simula language was nonsensically postponed for sensible use.

2.3 C with classes

"C with Classes" was the earlier version of C++. C++ got evolved through it. The main purposeof C with classes was to add classes in to the language. This work happened in between 1979-1983. This work determines the shape of C++.

The work, on what finally became C++, started with an undertaking to analyze the UNIX partto choose the amount it might be passed on over an association of laptops related by an area.This work started in April of 1979 in the Figuring Science Exploration Focus of bell Labs in Murray Slope, New Jersey, the started forward. Two subproblems after a short time emerged: how to examine the association traffic that would result from the piece movement and how to modularize the part. Both required a way to deal with impart the module plan of a perplexing structure and the correspondence illustration of the modules. This was overall such an issue that had become concluded never to attack again without real instruments. Consequently, the development of a genuine contraption according to the models that wereoutlined in Cambridge.

During the April to October period the advancement from thinking about a "gadget" to contemplating a "language" had occurred, yet C with Classes was at this point considered ona very basic level as a growth to C for conveying estimated quality and synchronization. A fundamental decision had been made, notwithstanding. Notwithstanding the way that help of concurrence and Simula-style reenactments was a fundamental place of C with Classes, thelanguage contained no locals for imparting concurrence; rather, a mix of heritage (class levelsof leadership) and the ability to portray class part works with outstanding ramifications saw by the preprocessor was used to create the library that maintained the ideal styles of synchronization. Mercifully note that "styles" is plural. I considered it basic, as I really do, thatmore than one thought of concurrence should be expressible in the language. This decision has been reconfirmed more than once by me and my partners, by other C++ customers, andby the C++ standards warning gathering. There are various applications for which maintain for concurrence is principal, yet there is no one winning model for synchronization maintain; hence when sponsorship is required it should be given through a library or a particular explanation increase with the objective that a particular sort of concurrence maintain doesn'thinder various constructions.

As such, the language gave general instruments to figuring everything out programs instead of help for express application zones. This was what made C with Classes, and later C++, an extensively valuable language rather than a C variety with expansions to help specific applications. A short time later, the choice between offering assistance for explicit applications or general thought frameworks, has come up more than once. Each time the decision has been to improve the reflection segments.

An early depiction of C with Classes was conveyed as a bell Labs particular report in April 1980[Stroustrup 1980a], and later in SIGPLAN Takes note. The SIGPLAN paper was in April 1982, followed by a more point by point Chime Labs specific report, "Adding Classes to the C Language: An Activity in Language Development" [Stroustrup 1982], that was thusly appropriated in Programming: Practice and Experience. These papers set a real model by portraying simply features that were totally executed and had been used. This was accordingto a long-standing act of bell Labs Figuring Science Exploration Center; that plan has been changed exactly where more openness about the inevitable destiny of C++ got expected to ensure a free and open conversation over the headway of C++ among its various non-AT&T customers.

C with Classes was explicitly expected to allow better relationship of activities; "estimation" was seen as an issue tended to by C. The expressing point was to facilitate with C in regard to run-time, code minimization, and data diminutiveness. In reality: someone once showed a three percent purposeful decrease in commonly run-time efficiency compared with C. This was seen as unsuitable and the overhead promptly disposed of. In like manner, to ensure design likeness with C and therefore avoid space overheads, no "housekeeping data" was placed in class objects.

Another critical concern was to avoid impediments on the space where C with Classes could be used. The ideal--which was cultivated - was that C with Classes could be used for whateverC could be used for. This proposed that just as organizing with C in efficiency, C with Classes couldn't offer advantages to the impediment of disposing of "dangerous" or "revolting" features of C. This discernment/standard should be repeated habitually to people (rare C withClasses customers) who required C with Classes made safer by growing static sort checking according to early Pascal. The elective technique for giving "security," embeddings run-time checks for each and every dangerous action, was (and is) considered reasonable for investigating conditions, at this point the language couldn't guarantee such checks without leaving C with a huge advantage in run-reality viability. Hence, such checks were not given for C Classes, anyway C++ conditions exist that give such checks to examining. Besides, customers can, and do, implant run-time checks (revelations [Stroustrup 1991]) where required and sensible.

C allows low-level errands, for instance, bit control and picking between different sizes of entire numbers. There are furthermore workplaces, as unequivocal unchecked sort changes, for deliberately breaking the sort structure, C with Classes, and later C++, follow this path byholding the low-level and perilous features of C. Instead of C, C++ intentionally discards the need to use such features beside where they are basic and performs hazardous undertakings exactly at the explicit request of the programmer. As every programmer have different stylesand ways to write a program and most certainly every problem have many ways to solve it so the language should be developed in a way so as to encourage a programmer to write his style out with only essentials of language to follow.

Features that were included in 1980:

1. Friend classes
2. Derived classes
3. Constructors and destructors

4. Public/private access control
5. Type checking and conversion of function arguments
6. Friend classes
7. Call and return functions (Section 15.2.4.8)

The features that they included into the language during 1981

8. Overloading of assignment operator
9. Default argument
10. Inline function

Since a preprocessor was used for the execution of C with Classes, simply new features, thatis, features not present in C, ought to have been depicted and the full power of C was direct open to customers. Both of these perspectives were esteemed by then. Having C as a subset fundamentally reduced the assistance and documentation work required. This was generallyhuge because for a serious drawn-out period of time I did the total of the C with Classes andlater C++ documentation and sponsorship just as doing the experimentation, plan, andexecution. Having all C features open additionally ensured that no requirements introduced through inclination or nonappearance of foresight on my part would prevent a customer from getting features viably open in C. Typically, convey ability to machines supporting C was ensured. From the start, C with Classes was done and used on a DEC PDP/11, yet soon it wasported to machines, for instance, DEC, VAX, and Motorola 68000-based machines. C with Classes was at this point seen as a vernacular of C. In addition, classes were insinuated as "A Theoretical Information Type Office for the C Language" [Stroustrup 1980a]. Support for object-orchestrated composing PC programs was not ensured until the course of action of virtual limits in C++ in 1983 [Stroustrup 1984a].

Key design decisions of that time:

1. C with Classes follows Simula in permitting the designer to decide types from which factors(objects) can be made, rather than, say, the Modula approach of showing a module as a grouping of articles and limits. In C with Classes (as in C++), a class is a sort, this is a fundamental thought in C++.

2. The depiction of objects of the customer portrayed sort is fundamental for the class introduction. This has broad consequences. For example, it suggests that certifiable area components can be done without the use of free store (load store, dynamic store) or refuse grouping. It moreover infers that a limit ought to be recompiled; the depiction of a thing it uses clearly is changed.

3. Gather time access control is used to bind permission to the depiction. As is normally done,only the limits referred to in the class confirmation can use names of class people. People

(when in doubt work people) showed in the public interface, the assertions after the public: name, can be used by other code.

4. The full kind (tallying both the return type and the conflict kinds) of a limit, is demonstrated for work people. Static (request time) type checking relies upon this benevolent detail. This changed from C by then, where work conflict types were neither decided in interfaces nor checked in calls.

5. Limit definitions are usually designated "elsewhere" to make a class more like an interfacespecific than a lexical instrument for figuring everything out source code. This gathers that extraordinary. This implies that separate accumulation for class part abilities and their clientsis simple and the linker period generally utilized for C is adequate to help C++.

6. The function new () is a constructor, a function with an uncommon which intends to the compiler. Such functions outfitted guarantees around directions. In this model, the assuranceis that the constructor, perceived actually confusingly as another trademark, on the time is destined to be alluded to as to introduce each object of its class before the primary utilizationof the object.

7. Both pointers and non-pointer types are provided (as in every C and Simula).

Much of the further improvements of C with classes and C++ may be viewed as investigating the consequences of these design decisions, misusing their proper components, and making up for the issues coming about because of their awful features. Many, besides in no way all, of the ramifications of those layout picks were perceived at that point; Stroustrup [1980a] is dated April 3, 1980. This level endeavors to make clear what changed into comprehended at the time and bring suggestions to segments clarifying later effects and acknowledge.

2.4 Run-Time Efficiency

The initial version of C with classes did not provide inline functions to take in addition benefit of the supply the illustration. Inline functions had been quickly provided, even though. The general purpose for the creation of inline functions became fear that the cost of crossing a protection barrier would possibly reason people to chorus from the use of commands to cover representation. Specially, Stroustrup [1982] observes that human beings had made records contributors public to avoid the function name overhead incurred with the useful resource of a constructor for simple schooling wherein most effective one or two assignments are needed for initialization. The instantaneous reason for the inclusion of inline capabilities into C with classes turned into a venture that could not control to pay for feature call overhead for a few commands involved in actual-time processing.

Over time, issues along those strains grew into the C++

"precept" that it became not so sufficient to offer a function, it had to be supplied in a less pricey form. Maximum really, "low fee" grow to be seen as that means "low-priced on hardware were common among developers" in area of "much less luxurious to researchers with excessive-quit device," or "low-cost in a couple of years while hardware can be less expensive." C with classes was continuously considered as a few things to be used now or subsequent month in choice as studies project to supply something in multiple years, therefore. In lining changed into taken into consideration critical for the application of education and, therefore, the difficultyemerge as more a way to offer it than whether or how not to offer it. Two arguments receivedthe day for the belief of getting the programmer pick out which functions the compiler needto attempt to inline.

The compiler best knows quality if it's been programmed to inline and it has a notion of time/space optimization that agrees with mine. The alternative languages become that most effective "the subsequent release" could actually inline and it might achieve this consistent with an inner good judgment that a programmer couldn't successfully manipulate. To make matters worse, C (and therefore, C with lessons and later C++) has authentic separate compilation in order that a compiler never has get admission to greater than a small a part ofthis system. In lining a function for which you don't know the supply seems feasible given advanced linker and optimizer technology, but such era wasn't to be had at the time (and still isn't in maximum environments).

2.5 The Linkage Model

The issue of the way one after the other compiled applications are connected together is vitalfor any programming language and, to a degree, determines the capabilities the language can provide. One of the crucial influences at the development of C with instructions and C++ wasthe choice that

1. Separate compilation ought to be possible with traditional C/FORTRAN UNIX/DOS fashionlinkers.
2. Linkage must in precept be kind secure.
3. Linkage must no longer require any form of database (even though one will be used toenhance a given implementation).
4. Linkage to software fragments written in other languages which include C, assembler, andFORTRAN have to be clean and green.

C makes use of "header documents" to ensure constant separate compilation. Declarations of facts structure layouts, capabilities, variables, and constants are located in header files which might be commonly textually blanketed into each supply record that wishes the declarations. Consistency is ensured through putting adequate information in the header files and making sure that the header documents are continuously protected. C++ follows this model up to some extent.

The purpose that format information may be found in a C++ class statement (although it doesn't have to be, is to make sure that the declaration and use of proper local variables is straightforward and efficient. As an instance:

```
Void func( )
{
 S
 t
 a
 c
 k
 s
 ;
 I
 n
 t
 c
 ;
 S
 .
 p
 u
 s
 h
 (
 '
 h
 '
 )
 ;
 C
 =
 s
 .
 p
```

```
o
p
(
)
;
}
```

Using the stack declaration, even a simple-minded C with lessons implementation can make certain that no need is fabricated from free shop for this situation, that the decision of dad (
) is in lined so that no function name overhead is incurred and that the non-in lined call of push ( ) can invoke a one by one compiled characteristic pop (). On this, C++ resembles Ada [Ichbiah 1979].

The concern for easy-minded implementations became partly a need due to the lack of assetsfor developing C with classes and partially a mistrust of languages and mechanisms that required "smart" strategies. An early components of a layout aim was that C with lessons "must be implementable without using an set of rules extra complicated than a linear seek."anyplace that rule of thumb turned into violated, as inside the case of feature overloading , it led to semantics that had been more complicated than each person felt at ease with and usually also to implementation headaches.

The intention--based totally on my Simula experience--became to design a language that would be easy sufficient to apprehend to attract customers and smooth sufficient to enforceto draw implementers. Only if a fairly simple implementation might be used by an enormouslynewbie user in a rather unsupportive programming surroundings to deliver code that as compared favorably with C code in improvement time, correctness, run-time velocity, and code length, ought to C with training, and later C++, anticipate to live to tell the tale in competition with C.

This changed into a part of a philosophy of fostering self-sufficiency among customers. The intention turned into continually and explicitly to develop neighborhood knowledge in all aspects of the use of C++. Most organizations should observe the exact opposite approach. They preserve customers dependent on offerings that generate sales for a critical assist company and/or consultant. In my view, this contrast is a deep cause for some of the variations between C++ and plenty of different languages.

The decision to work in the pretty primitive and nearly universally available framework of the C linking centers triggered the essential trouble that a C++ compiler must continually paintings with handiest partial records approximately a software. An assumption made about a software ought to likely be violated via a program written the next day in a few other language(inclusive of C, FORTRAN, or assembler) and related in probable after this system has commenced executing. This trouble surfaces in many contexts. It's far tough for an implementation to assure

1. That something is unique,
2. That (kind) information is constant,
3. That something is initialized.

In addition, C offers handiest and feeblest guide for the perception of separate name spacesin order that fending off name space pollutants by way of one at a time written program segments becomes a trouble. Over the years, C++ has tried to stand all of these demanding situations without departing from the essential model and generation that gives portability, but within the C with training days we simply relied on the C technique of header documents.Through the popularity of the C linker got here every other "principle" for the development of C++: C++ is just one language in a system and not a complete device. In different phrases, C++ accepts the function of a traditional programming language with a fundamental difference among the language, the running machine, and other vital elements of the programmer's international. This delimits the position of the language in a way this is difficultto do for a language, inclusive of Smalltalk or Lisp, that became conceived as an entire gadget or environment. It makes it critical that a C++ software fragment can name program fragments written in other languages and that a C++ software fragment can itself be referredto as by means of software fragments written in other languages. Being "just a language" additionally allows C++ implementations to gain immediately from equipment written for different languages.

The need for a programming language and the code written in it to be only a cog in a miles larger gadget is of maximum significance to most business customers, yet such co-existence with other languages and systems was apparently not a primary problem to most theoreticians, might-be perfectionists, and academic users. It was the main reason for the success of C++.

2.6 Static Type Checking

To keep the C code away from breaking, it turned into decided to allow the call of an undeclared feature and not carry out type checking on such undeclared features. This became of path a main hollow in the type machine, and several attempts had been made to decrease its importance because the foremost occurrence of programming errors before in the end, in C++, the hollow was closed by using creating a call of an undeclared characteristic unlawful. One simple commentary defeated all tries to compromise, and as a result keep a greater diploma of C compatibility: As programmers found out C with training, they misplaced the capacity to find run-time errors as a result of simple type errors. Having come to depend on the sort checking and type conversion furnished by means of C with instructions or C++, they lost the capacity to quickly locate the "silly mistakes" that creep into C packages via the lack of checking. Similarly, they didn't take the precautions towards such silly errors that exact C programmers take as a count of path. After all, "such errors do not take place in C with training." for that reason, as the frequency of run-time mistakes caused by uncaught argument kind mistakes is going down, their seriousness and the time needed to discover them goes up. The result turned into critically annoyed programmers worrying similarly tightening of the kind machine.

The maximum thrilling test with "incomplete static checking" became the method of permitting calls of undeclared features but noting the type of the arguments used in order that a consistency test will be completed when in addition calls have been visible. Whilst Walter brilliant many years later independently discovered this trick, he named it "auto prototyping," the usage of the ANSI C term prototype for a function assertion. The revel in turned into that auto prototyping stuck many mistakes and to begin with multiplied aprogrammer's self-belief within the type machine. However, on the grounds that regular errors and mistakes in a characteristic known as simplest once in a compilation had been now not stuck, auto prototyping ultimately destroyed programmer confidence within the type checker and precipitated a feel of paranoia even worse than that was witnessed in C or BCPLprogrammers.

C with lessons brought the notation f (void) for a characteristic f that takes no arguments as a comparison to f ( ) that in C announces a function that could take any quantity of arguments of any type with none type test. My users soon convinced me, but, that the f (void) notation wasn't very fashionable, and that having functions declared f ( ) be given arguments wasn't very intuitive. Consequently, the end result of the experiment changed into to have f ( ) suggest a characteristic f that takes no arguments, as any beginner might count on. It took support from each Doug mciiroy and Dennis Ritchie for me to build up braveness to make thisdamage from C. Most effective when they used the phrase abomination approximately f (void) did I dare provide f ( ) the apparent which means. However, to this day C's kind regulations are a great deal laxer than C++'s and any use of f ( ) as a characteristic statementbetween the Two languages is incompatible.

2.7 Syntax Problem

In C, the call of a shape, a "shape tag," should continually be preceded with the aid of the key-word struct. For instance

Struct buffer a;   /* 'struct' is vital in C */

In the context of C with classes, this had annoyance for some time as it made user-described kinds second kind residents syntactically. The call of a struct or a category is now a type call and requires no unique syntactic identity:

Buffer a;   // C++

The ensuing fights over C compatibility lasted for years.

2.8 Derived Classes

The C with classes concept becomes supplied without any shape of run-time support. In particular, the Simula (and C++) concept of a virtual function became missing. The reason for this turned into the purpose, of educating human beings how to use them and, even extra, the persuasion of people that a virtual feature is as green in time and area as an everyday characteristic, as usually used. Often human beings with Simula and Smalltalk revel innonetheless don't quite believe that until they've had the C++ implementation explained to them in element--and plenty of still harbor irrational doubts after that.

Even without virtual capabilities, derived lessons in C with classes have been beneficial for constructing new statistics systems out of antique ones and for associating operations with the resulting sorts. In particular, as explained in Stroustrup [1980] and Stroustrup [1982], theyallowed list lessons to be defined, and also task training.

In the absence of digital capabilities, a consumer may want to use gadgets of a derived elegance and treat base instructions as implementation info (only). Alternatively, a specific kind field may be introduced in a base class and used together with express kind casts. The previous approach changed into used for responsibilities where the user handiest sees particular derived venture classes and "the system" sees most effective the undertaking basetraining. The latter approach was used for diverse software instructions wherein, in impact, a base magnificence turned into used to put in force a variant report for a hard and fast of derived training. A great deal of the effort in C with instructions and later C++ has been to make certain that programmers need not write such code.

2.9 Protection Model

Function were made to be able to declare in public parts of the class or by specifying a function or a category as a friend. Initially, simplest instructions may be pals, consequently granting get right of entry to all member features of the friend magnificence, but later it turned into observed handy so that it will grant get right of entry to (friendship) to individualfeatures. Specifically, it changed into found useful if you want to furnish get entry to global functions. A friendship declaration turned into seen as a mechanism much like that of one safety domain granting a study-write capability to some other.

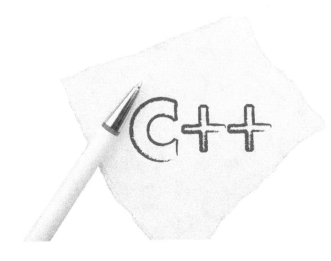

2.10 Run-Time Guarantees

The access control mechanisms defined above honestly prevent unauthorized get right of entry to. A second form of guarantee supplied by "special member features," which includesconstructors, that have been identified and implicitly invoked through the compiler. The idea was to permit the programmer to establish guarantees, once in a while called "invariants," that different member functions may want to rely upon. Curiously sufficient, the preliminary implementation contained a feature that isn't always provided via C++ but is regularly asked. In C with lessons, it became feasible to define a characteristic that might implicitly be knownas earlier than each name of every member function (except the constructor) and another that might be implicitly referred to as earlier than every return from every member function. They were called call and return functions. They were used to provide synchronization for themonitor class inside the original task library [Stroustrup 1980b]:

Class monitor: object
{
/* ... */
C
a
l
l
(
)
(
/
*
p
i
c
k
l
o
c
k
*

```
/
)
R
e
t
u
r
n
(
)
(
.
/
*
r
e
l
e
a
s
e
l
o
c
k
*
/
)
}:
```

These are comparable in cause to the CLOS: before and: after methods. Name and return capabilities were eliminated from the language due to the fact no person used them and because no one persuaded human beings that call and return functions had essential uses. In 1987, Mike Tiemann cautioned an alternative solution known as "wrappers" [Tiemann 1987].

Chapter 3

3.1 From C with Classes to C++

Throughout 1982, it became clear that C with classes became a "medium success" and might remain so till it died. So, a medium was defined for fulfillment as something so beneficial that it without problems paid for itself and its developer, but not so attractive and beneficial that it'd pay for a help and improve organization. Accordingly, persevering with C with classes and its C preprocessor implementation would condemn to aid C with classes' use indefinitely. So, there were only two methods derived out of this dilemma:

1. Stop supporting C with classes, in order that the customers could need to pass elsewhere.

2. Develop a new and better language based on my experience with C with classes that would serve a huge sufficient set of users to pay for aid and development enterprise hence at that time it was observed that 5000 commercial users are essential minimum.

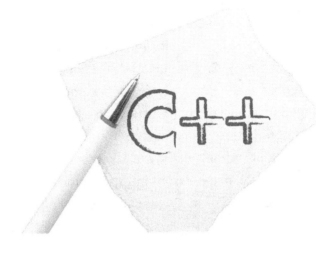

The success of C with classes became an easy outcome of
assembly its layout purpose: C with instructions did help
arrange a large elegance of applications considerably higher
than C, without the lack of run-time performance and without
requiring enough cultural adjustments to make its use
unfeasible in groups that had been unwilling to undergo
foremost changes. The elements restricting its success have
been partially the limited set of latest facilities presented over
C, and partially the preprocessor generation used to implement
C with lessons. There simply wasn't sufficient assist in C with
classes for individuals who have been willing to invest
tremendous efforts to acquire matching advantages: C with
classes become a vital step in the proper route, but simplest
one small step.

The resulting language was at the start nonetheless referred to
as C with lessons, however after a polite request from control

it changed into given the name C84. The motive for the naming becomes that people had taken to calling C with classes "new C," after which C. This closing abbreviation caused C being known as "simple C," "immediately C," and "vintage C." The call C84 turned into used only for a few months, partially as it changed into unsightly andinstitutional, in part because there would nonetheless be confusion if humans dropped the "84." ideas for a brand-new call were asked and picked C++ because it became brief, had pleasant interpretations, and wasn't of the form "adjective C." In C, ++ can, depending on context, be examine as "next," "successor," or "increment," even though it's far usually suggested "plus". The call C++ and its runner up ++C are fertile assets for jokes and puns-- almost all of which had been regarded and favored before the name become chosen. The callC++ turned into cautioned by Rick Mascitti. It changed into first used in Stroustrup [1984b] wherein it become edited into the final copy in December 1983.

3.2 Cfront

The Cfront compiler front-end for the C84 language changed into designed and carried out via me between the spring of 1982 and the summer time of 983. The primary person outside the computer science research center, Jim Coplien, obtained his replica in July of 1983. Jim changed into in a group that were doing experimental switching paintings with C with Classes in Bell Labs in Naperville, Illinois, for some time.

In that equal time period designed C84, drafted the reference guide published January 1, 1984[Stroustrup 1984a], designed the complicated variety library and implemented it, collectively with Eeonie Rose[Rose]984], designed and implemented the first string class together with Jonathan Shopiro, maintained and ported the C with classes implementation, and supported the C with classes customers and helped them grow to be C84 users. Cfront turned into (and is) a traditional compiler the front-end, performing a whole take a look at of the syntax and semantics of the language, building an inner representation of its input, reading and rearranging that illustration, and subsequently producing output suitable for a few code generators. The internal illustration changed into (is) a graph with one symbol table in keeping with scope. The overall strategy is to study a supply document one worldwide statement at a time and bring output handiest when a whole global declaration has been completely analyzed.

The agency of Cfront is reasonably traditional, besides perhaps for the use of many symbol tables instead of just one. Cfront become at the beginning written in C with Classes and soon transcribed into C84 so that the very first running C++ compiler turned into executed in C++. Even the first model of Cfront used classes heavily, however no virtual capabilities because they were not available at the project start.

The maximum uncommon for its time issue of Cfront become that it generated C code. This has brought on no cease of confusion. Cfront generated C due to the fact. Ought to easily have generated some inner back-give up format or assembler from Cfront, however that turned into not what customers wanted. In reaction to this need, concluded that using C as a common input format to a massive variety of code turbines became the only reasonable preference. The strategy of constructing a compiler as a C generator has later become prettypopular, in order that languages consisting of Ada, CLOS, Eiffel, Modula-three, and Smalltalk have been applied that way. C compiler is used as a code generator most effective. Any mistakes message from the C compiler reflects a mistake inside the C compiler or in Cfront, however no longer within the C++ source textual content. Every syntactic and semantic blunder is in precept caught by usingCfront, the C++ compiler front-give up. There has been a protracted history of bewildermentabout what Cfront changed into/is. It's been known as a preprocessor because it generates C,and for humans within the C network (and some other place) that has been taken as evidencethat Cfront changed into an alternatively easy program something like a macro preprocessor.Humans have accordingly "deduced" (wrongly) that a line-for-line translation from C++ to C is possible, that symbolic debugging at the C++ level is impossible when Cfront is used, that code generated by using Cfront should be not so good as code generated with the aid of "actual compilers," that C++ wasn't a "actual language," and so on.

Cfront is just a compiler front-end and can by no means be used for real programming itself.It uses a driver force to run the source document through the C preprocessor, Cpp, then run the output of Cpp through Cfront, and the output from Cfront through a C compiler:

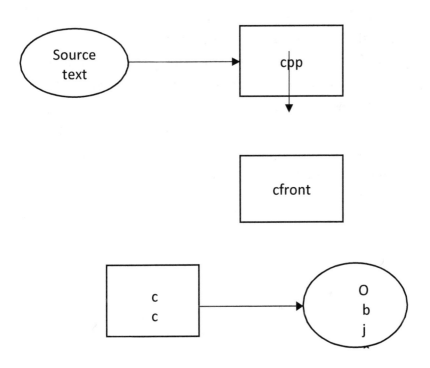

Similarly, the driver ought to make certain that dynamic (run-time) initialization is carried out. In Cfront 3.0, the driver became but extra intricate as automated template instantiation.

As stated, it was decided to stay within the constraints of traditional linkers. But there was one constraint that was felt too tough to live with: most traditional linkers had a very low restriction on the variety of characters that may be used in external names. A limit of 8 characters changed into not unusual, and 6 characters and one case most effective are guaranteed to work as outside names in Classical C; ANSI/ISO C accepts that restrict also. For the reason that the call of a member feature includes the name of its class and that the type of an overloaded characteristic needs to be meditated inside the linkage manner in some way or other. Cfront uses encodings to enforce type safe linkage in a way that makes a restriction of 32 characters too low for comfort and even 256 is a piece tight at instances. Within the meantime, systems of hash coding of long identifiers were used with archaic linkers, but that turned into by no means completely great.

Versions of C++ are often named by means of Cfront launch numbers. Launch 1.0 was the language as described in "The C++ Programming Language".

Releases 1.1 (June 1986) and 1.2 (February 1987) had been typically bug restoration releaseshowever also introduced hints to individuals and guarded contributors. Release 2.0 become a primary clean-up that still brought multiple inheritance in June 1989. Release 2.1 (April 1990) changed into more often than not a computer virus restore release that introduced Cfront (nearly) into line with the definition within the ARM. Release 3.0 (September 1991) delivered templates as detailed within the ARM. Launch 4.0 is predicted to feature exceptiondealing with as distinctive within the ARM.

3.3 Language Feature Details

1. References
2. Function name and operator overloading
3. Virtual functions
4. Improved type checking
5. User-controlled free-store memory control
6. Constants (const)

3.4 Virtual Functions

The most obvious new characteristic in C++, and clearly the one that had the finest impact onthe fashion of programming one should use for the language, was virtual functions. The idea become borrowed from Simula and presented in a shape that intended to make easy and efficient implementation.

The motive for virtual functions was presented in Stroustrup [1986b] and [1986c]. To emphasize the important position of virtual capabilities in C++ programming, i can be quote:"An abstract data type defines a form of black box. As soon as it's been described, it does nownot truly interact with the rest of the program. There's no way of adapting it to new uses except via modifying its definition. This could cause severe inflexibility. Keep in mind defininga type form for use in a portrait's device. Count on for the instant that the system has to aid circles, triangles, and squares. Expect additionally that you have a few classes:

C
l
a
s
s
p
o
i
n
t

/
*
.
.
.
*
/
)
;
C
l
a
s
s
c
o
l
o
r
/
*
.
.
.
*
/
;
You might
outline a
shape like
this: Enum

```
kind (
circle,
triangle,
rectangula
r };Class
shape (
point
center;
Color col;
```

Kind k;
/
/
r
e
p
r
e
s
e
n
t
a
t
i
o
n
o
f
s
h
a
p
e
P
u
b
l
i
c
:

```
Point where () ( return center; }
Void move (point to)  {center = to; draw();
)
V
o
i
d
d
r
a
w
(
)
;
V
o
i
d
r
o
t
a
t
e
(
i
n
t
)
;
// extra operations
```

};

The "type field" k is important to permit operations which include draw ( ) and rotate
Of shape they are managing (in a Pascal-like language, one would possibly use a variant recordwith tag k). The function draw ( ) is probably described like this:

V
o
i
d
s
h
a
p
e
:
:
d
r
a
w
(
)
{
S
w
i
t
c

h
(
k
)
{
c
a
s
e
c
i
r
c
l
e
:
/
/
d
r
a
w
a
c
i
r
c
l
e
B
r

e
a
k
;
c
a
s
e
t
r
i
a
n
g
l
e
:
/
/
d
r
a
w
a
t
r
i
a
n
g
l

```
e
b
r
e
a
k
;
C
a
s
e
s
q
u
a
r
e
:
// draw a square
}}
```

This is a large number. Capabilities along with draw ( ) have to "know about" all the sorts of shapes there are. Consequently, the code for this type of characteristic grows every time a brand-new shape is brought to the device. If you define a brand-new shape, every operationon a shape have to be tested and (probably) modified. You aren't able to upload a new shape to a device except you have got get entry to the supply code for every operation. Because adding a brand-new form entails "touching" the code of every essential operation on shapes,it requires awesome skill set and potentially introduces bugs into the code dealing with other (older) shapes. The choice of illustration of precise shapes can get significantly cramped through the requirement that (as a minimum a number of) their representation should suit into the normally constant sized framework presented through the definition of the overall kind shape.

The Simula inheritance mechanism presents a solution. First, specify a class that defines the general properties of all shapes:

C
l
a
s
s
s
h
a
p
e
{
p
o
i
n
t
c
e
n
t
e
r

```
;
C
o
l
o
r
c
o
l
;
// ... Public :
```

```
Point where() { return center; }
Void move(point to) { center =
to; draw(); ) virtual void draw();
Virtual void rotate (int) ;
// ...
};
```

The functions for which the calling interface may be described, however where the implementation cannot be described besides for a selected shape, had been marked "digital"(the Simula and C++ time period for "can be redefined later in a category derived from this one"). Given this definition, standard capabilities manipulating shapes were written:

```
Void rotate_all(shape** v, int size, int angle)
// rotate all members of vector "v"
of size "size" "angle" degrees (For
(int i = O; i < size; i++) v[i]
.rotate(angle);
```

)

To outline a particular shape, we have to say that it is a shape and specify its particular properties (which includes the virtual function):

C
l
a
s
s
c
i
r
c
l
e
:
p
u
b
l
i
c
s
h
a
p
e
(

I
n
t
r
a
d
i
u
s
;
p
u
b
l
i
c
:

```
Void draw ( ) { /* ... */ };
Void rotate(int) {} // yes, the null function};
```

In C++, c1 as circle is said to be derived from class shape, and class shape is said to be a baseof class circle. An alternative terminology calls circle and shape subclass and superclass, respectively.

The key implementation concept became that the set of virtual functions in a category definesan array of pointers to functions, in order that a name of a digital characteristic is virtually an oblique characteristic name thru that array. There is one array in step per class and one pointer to such an array in every object of a class that has virtual functions.

Designed software wouldn't want the extensibility and openness provided by using virtual functions, in order that right evaluation might show which non-virtual functions will be referred to as at once. Therefore, the argument went, virtual functions have been actually a shape of inefficiency. But virtual functions were added in the language anyway.

3.5 Overloading

Several human beings had requested for the capacity to overload operators. Reluctant pointsto not to add overloading in C++:

1. Overloading become reputed to be tough to enforce so that compilers would grow totremendous size.
2. Overloading was reputed to be tough to educate and hard to outline precisely in orderthat manuals and tutorials would develop to giant length.
3. Code written the use of operator overloading became reputed to be inherently inefficient.
4. Overloading changed into reputed to make code incomprehensible.

If all of these conjectures were false, then overloading might remedy some real problems forC++ users. There had been folks that would really like to have complex numbers, matrices, and APL-like vectors in C++. There were folks that would really like range-checked arrays, multi-dimensional arrays, and strings in C++. There have been at the least two separate programs for which people desired to overload logical operators which includes I(or), & (and),and ^ (distinctive or). The way I saw it, the listing turned into long and might grow with the scale and the variety of the C++ consumer populace. My answer to [4], "overloading makes code difficult to understand," become that several of the programmers, whose opinions werevalued and whose experience became measured in many years, claimed that their code would become cleaner in the event that they had overloading. So, what if you'll write difficult to understand code with overloading? It's miles possible to put in writing obscure code in any language. Its topics extra how a feature may be used properly than how it could be misused.First it was discovered that use of class with over-loaded operators, such as complex and string, changed into pretty easy and didn't placed a main burden at the programmer. Subsequent a guide released, the guide sections to prove that the delivered complexity wasn'ta serious problem; the forty-two-page manual needed less than a page and a half more. So, the first implementation in hours using most effective 18 strains of extra code in Cfront.

Certainly, these kinds of problems were not genuinely tackled in this strict sequential order. But, the focal point of the paintings did begin with application issues and slowly drifted to implementation troubles.

In retrospect, the complexity of the definition and implementation problems and compounded these troubles by seeking to isolate overloading mechanisms from the relaxation of the language semantics. The latter become done out of erroneous worry of perplexing customers.

Overload print ( ) ;

Should precede declarations of an overloaded
function print, which includesVoid print(int) ;
Void print (const char*) ;

Additionally, insisted that ambiguity manipulate should take place in two stages so that resolutions concerning built-in operators and conversions would constantly take precedence over resolutions related to person-defined operations. Maybe the latter changed into inevitable, given the priority for C compatibility and the chaotic nature of the C conversion regulations for built-in types. These conversions do now not constitute a lattice; for instance, implicit conversions are allowed each from into to drift and from waft to int. But, the policiesfor ambiguity resolution have been too complicated, triggered surprises, and needed to be revised for launch 2.0.

Requiring express overload declarations become undeniable wrong and the requirement become dropped in release 2.0.

3.6 References

References had been delivered basically to aid operator overloading. C passes each function argument by means of value, and in which passing an object by using value might beinefficient or beside the point the user can bypass a pointer. This strategy doesn't work whereoperator overloading is used. If so, notational comfort is vital so that a user can't anticipate to insert address of operators if the objects are massive.

Troubles with debugging ALGOL 68 convinced that having references that did not trade whatobject they stated after initialization, was an excellent component. Due to the fact C++ has each recommendations and references, it does not want operations for distinguishing operations at the reference itself from operations on the object cited (like Simula), or the sortof deductive mechanism hired by using ALGOL 68.

It's essential that const references can be initialized by way of non-lvalues and lvalues of types that require conversion. Specifically, that is what lets in a FORTRAN feature to be referred toas with a steady:

Extern "Fortran" go with the " float sqrt (const flow&); // °&' means reference sqrt(2); // callby way of reference

Jonathan Shopiro was deeply worried inside the discussions

that brought about the introduction of references. Similarly, to the obvious makes use of references, together with argument, taken into consideration the ability to apply references as return sorts critical. Thisallowed to have a very simple index operator for a string class:

```
Class String { // ...
Char& operator [] (int index); // subscript operator // return a reference
};
Void f(String& s)
{
Char cl = ...
S[i] = cl; //
assign to
operator [] 's
result // ...
Char c2 = s[i];
// assign
operator [] 's
result
}
```

The consideration permitting separate features for left-hand and right-hand side use of afeature but considered the use of references the easier opportunity, even though this implied to introduce extra "helper classes" to resolve a few issues where returning a simple referencewasn't sufficient.

3.7 Constants (const)

In operating systems, it's far common to have get access to a few pieces of memory controlled without delay or circuitously through bits: one which indicates whether or not a user can writeto it and one that shows whether a user can read it. This concept appeared without delay relevant to C++ and [taken into consideration allowing every kind to be distinctive read onlyor write only. The notion is focused on specifying interfaces instead of on offering symbolic constants for C. Clearly, a read-only value is a symbolic constant, but the scope of the conceptis far greater. To start with, it was proposed to read-only but now not read-only pointers. Sometime later, the ANSI C committee (X3J]!) Was formed and the const proposal resurfacedthere and have become a part of ANSI/[SO C.

But, within the interim [had experimented similarly with const in C with lessons anddiscovered that const become a beneficial opportunity to macros for representing constantsbest if an international consts were implicitly local to their compilation unit. Best if so, shouldthe compiler without problems deduce that their value truly did not alternate and allow simple consts in steady reviews and for that reason avoid allocating space for such constantsand use them in constant expressions. C did no longer undertake this rule. This makes constsfar less useful in C than in C++ and leaves C depending on the preprocessor in which C++ programmers can use nicely typed and scoped consts.

3.8 Memory Management

Long earlier the primary C with classes program was written, Bjarne Stroustrup knew that free store (dynamic memory) would be used extra closely in a language with classes than in traditional C programs. This turned into the reason for the introduction of the new and deleteoperators in C with Classes. The new operator that each allocates memory from the free storeand invokes a constructor to ensure initialization turned into borrowed from Simula. The delete operator was a necessary complement because Bjarne Stroustrup did not want C withlessons to rely on a garbage collector. The argument for the new operator may be summarizedlike this. Could you rather write:

```
X* p = new X(2);
Struct X * p =
(struct X *)
malloc(sizeof(struc
t X));If (p == O)
error("memory
exhausted");
P->init (2) ;
```

And in which version are you maximum likely to make a screw up? The arguments towards it,which had been voiced pretty much load at the time, have been "however we don't actually need it," and "but a person can have used new as an identifier." both observations are correct, of course.

Introducing "operator new" for this reason made the use of free save extra convenient and much less errors prone. This expanded its use even in addition so that the C free store allocation habitual m a l l o c ( ) used to enforce new became the most not unusual overall performance bottleneck in actual systems. This turned into no real wonder both; the only hassle become what to do approximately it. Having real packages spend 50 percentage or more in their time in malloc ( ) wasn't desirable.

Bjarne Stroustrup discovered consistent with-class allocators and deallocators very powerful. The fundamental idea is that free store memory usage is dominated by way of the allocation and deallocation of plenty of small gadgets from only a few instructions. Take over the allocation of those items in a separate allocator and you can shop both time and space for those objects and also lessen the quantity of fragmentation of the overall free store. The mechanism provided for 1.0, "assignments to this," changed into too low level and error prone and turned into changed with the aid of a cleaner solution in 2.0.

Observe that static and automatic (stack allotted) objects had been continually feasible and that the only memory control strategies relied closely on such objects. The string class became a standard example; here string objects are normally on the stack in order that they require no explicit memory management, and the free store they depend on is controlled completely and invisibly to the user with the aid of the String member functions.

3.9 Type Checking

The C++ kind checking rules were the result of experiments with the C with classes. All characteristic calls are checked at bring together time. The checking of trailing arguments can be suppressed through explicit specification in a feature statement. That is crucial to allow C'sprint f ():

```
Int printf(const char* ...) ;
// accept any argument after
// the initial character string
// ...
Printf("date: %s %d 19%d\n", month, day, year); // maybe right
```

Numerous mechanisms have been supplied to relieve the withdrawal signs and symptoms that many C programmers feel when they first revel in strict checking. Overriding kind checking using the ellipsis changed into the most drastic and least advocated of these. Characteristic name overloading and default arguments [Stroustrup 1986b] made it possible to provide the arrival of a single function taking a selection of argument lists withoutcompromising type safety. The stream I/O system demonstrates that the weak checking wasn't essential even for I/O.

Chapter 4

4.1 C++ 2.0

Now (mid 1986), the direction for C++ become set for all who cared to see. The important thing design decisions were made. The course of the destiny evolution become for parameterized types, multiple inheritance, and exception handling. Tons experimentation and adjustment based totally on experience was needed, however the glory days had been over. C++ had by no means been stupid putty, however, there has been now no realopportunity for radical change. For suitable and horrific, what become carried out become accomplished. What become left turned into a super quantity of strong work. At this point C++ had about 2,000 users international.

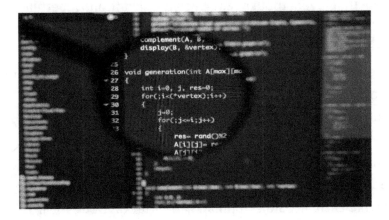

This was the factor in which the plan as at first conceived by way of Steve Johnson and BjarneStroustrup was for a development and support organization to take over the everyday work at the tools (in general Cfront), for that reason releasing Bjarne Stroustrup to work on the new functions and the libraries that had been expected to depend upon them. This become additionally the factor in which Bjarne Stroustrup predicted first AT&T, and then others, couldbegin to construct compilers and different tools to ultimately make Cfront redundant.

Virtually, they had already started, but the precise plan turned into soon derailed due to management indecisiveness, ineptness, and absence of focus. A project to develop a trendy C++ compiler diverted interest and resources from Cfront protection and improvement. A plan to ship a release 1.3 in early 1988 absolutely fell thru the cracks. The net impact becomethat they had to wait until June of 1989 for launch 2.0, and that even though 2.0 become significantly better than release 1.2 in almost all ways, 2.0 did not provide the language capabilities mentioned inside the "whatis paper," and therefore a substantially progressed and prolonged library wasn't part of it.

Some of the folks who prompted C with classes and the original C++ endured to assist with the evolution in diverse methods. Phil Brown, Tom Cargill, Jim Coplien, Steve Dewhurst, Keith Gorlen, Laura Eaves, Bob Kelley, Brian Kernighan, Andy Koenig, Archie Lachner, Stan Lippman,Larry Mayka, Doug McIlroy, Pat Philip, Dave Prosser, Peggy Quinn, Roger Scott, Jerry Schwarz, Jonathan Shopiro, and Kathy Stark were explicitly recounted in [Stroustrup 1989b].

Stability of the language definition and its implementation

78

become taken into consideration important. The functions of 2.0 have been fairly simple modifications of the language primarily based on experience in with the 1. * releases. The maximum important element oflaunch 2.0 changed into that it multiplied the generality of the individual language features and advanced their integration into the language.

4.2 Feature Overview

1. Better resolution of overloaded functions.

2. Recursive definition of assignment and initialization
3. Multiple inheritance
4. Type-safe linkage
5. Abstract classes
6. Better facilities for user-defined memory management
7. P r o t e c t e d members (first provided in release 1.2)
8. Pointers to members (first provided in release 1.2)
9. Static member functions,
10. Overloading of operator ->, and
11. Const member functions

Maximum of those extensions and refinements represented experience won with C++ and could not have been added earlier without greater foresight than Bjarne Stroustrup possessed. Evidently, integrating these functions involved full work, but it become very unlucky that this became allowed to take precedence over the completion of the language as outlined in the "whatis" paper.

Most capabilities enhanced the protection of the language in some way or different. Cfront

2.0 checked the consistency of characteristic sorts throughout separate compilation units (type safe linkage), made the overload resolution guidelines order independent, and also ensured that greater calls have been taken into consideration ambiguous. The notion of constwas made extra comprehensive, and pointers to members closed a loophole within the type system and provided explicit class-specific memory allocation and deallocation operations to make the error-susceptible "assignment to this" technique redundant.

To a few people, the most critical "feature" of release 2.0 wasn't a feature in any sense but asimple space optimization.

From the start, the code generated with the aid of Cfront tended to be pretty suitable. As late as 1992, Cfront generated the fastest strolling code in a benchmark used to assess C++ compilers on a Sparc. There were no tremendous improvements in Cfront's code era because launch 1.0. However, launch 1. * changed into wasteful because every compilation unit generated its personal set of digital feature tables for all the lessons utilized in that unit. This could result in megabytes of waste. At the time (approximately 1984), Bjarne Stroustrup considered the waste essential within the absence of linker guide and asked for such linker assist. By means of 1987 that linker support hadn't materialized. Therefore, Bjarne Stroustrup re-thought the problem and solved it by the simple heuristic of laying down the virtual characteristic table of a category right next to its first non-digital non-inline function.

4.3 Multiple Inheritance

In most of the people's minds, a couple of inheritance, the ability to have or more direct baseclasses, is the function of 2.0. Bjarne Stroustrup disagreed on the time because Bjarne Stroustrup felt that the sum of the upgrades to the sort device have been of far more sensible importance. Also, adding a couple of inheritance in 2.0 changed into a mistake. More than one inheritance belongs in C++ however is a way less critical than parameterized sorts. Because it passed off, parameterized types inside the form of templates handiest regarded in release 3.0. There had been more than one reasons for deciding on to work on multiple inheritance at the time: The design became further superior and the implementation could be achieved within Cfront. Every other thing turned into simply irrational. Nobody doubted that Bjarne Stroustrup should put in force templates successfully. Hence multiple inheritance, however, become extensively speculated to be very hard to implement correctly. For that reason, multiple inheritance seemed extra of an undertaking, and due to the fact Bjarne Stroustrup had taken into consideration it as early as 1982 and located an easy and efficient implementation method in 1984, Bjarne Stroustrup could not face up to the mission. I suspect that that is the handiest case in which style affected the series of events.

In September of 1984, Bjarne Stroustrup supplied the C++ operator overloading mechanism at the IFIP WG2.four conference in Canterbury [Stroustrup 1984c]. There Bjarne Stroustrup met Stein Krogdahl from the university of Oslo who became just completing an offer for adding multiple inheritance to Simula [Krogdahl 1984]. His thoughts became the basis for the implementation of regular a couple of base lessons in C++. He and that Bjarne Stroustrup later discovered out that the thought become almost identical to an idea for providing multiple inheritance in Simula that were taken into consideration by way of Ole-Johan Dahl in 1966 and rejected because it might have complicated the Simula rubbish collector [Dahl 1988].

The unique and essential purpose for thinking about a couple of inheritance changed into virtually to permit training to be blended into one in this kind of way that items of the resulting class would behave as items of either base class [Stroustrup 1986c]:

A fairly fashionable example of the usage of multiple inheritance might be to provide library classes displayed and task for representing items under the control of a show manager and co-routine under the control of a scheduler, respectively. A programmer ought to then createlessons such as

Class my_displayed task : public displayed, public task { // ...
};
Class my_task : public task { // not displayed // ...
};
Class my_displayed : public displayed { // not a task // ...
};

The usage of (simplest) single inheritance handiest of those three alternatives would be opento the programmer.

The implementation requires little greater than remembering the relative offsets of the Cask and displayed objects in a my_displayed_task object. All the gory implementation info had been defined in Stroustrup [1987a]. Similarly, the language layout ought to specify how ambiguities are treated and what to do if a class is special as a base magnificence extra thanas soon as in a derived class:

Ambiguities am handled ~ compile time:

```
Class A { public: void f(); /* ... */ };
Class B { public: void f(); /* ... */ };
Class C
:public A,
public B { /*
no f() ... */ };
Void g() { C*
p;
P->f(); // error: ambiguous }
```

In this, C++ differs from the item-oriented Lisp dialects that support multiple inheritance. Basically, Bjarne Stroustrup rejected all types of dynamic resolution past using virtual featuresas incorrect for a statically typed language under extreme efficiency constraints. Maybe,Bjarne Stroustrup must at this factor have revived the notion of call 1 and return functionsto mimic the CLOS: before and : after methods. But human beings were already traumaticabout the complexity of the multiple inheritance mechanisms and i am continually reluctantto re-open old wounds.

A couple of inheritance in C++ became debatable [Cargill 1991; Carroll 1991; Waldo 1991; Sakkinen 1992] for several motives. The arguments against it targeted across the real and imaginary complexity of the concept, the utility of the idea, and the effect of more than one inheritance on other extensions and tool building. Further, proponents of more than one inheritance can, and do, argue over exactly what more than one inheritance is meant to be and the way its miles quality supported in a language. I assume, as I did then, that the essentialflaw in these arguments is that they take more than one inheritance far too significantly. Multiple inheritance would not resolve all your troubles; however, it doesn't need to becauseit is pretty cheap, and from time to time it is very convenient to have. Grady sales space [Booch 1991] expresses a slightly more potent sentiment: "more than one inheritance is likea parachute, you do not want it very often, however while you do it's essential."

4.4 Abstract Classes

The final feature delivered to 2.0 earlier than it shipped turned into virtual. Past due change to releases are never famous and overdue changes to the definition of what will be shipped are even less so. Bjarne Stroustrup understood that several individuals of control concept I had lost touch with the real global when I insisted on this selection.

A commonplace criticism about C++ turned into (and is) that private data is seen and that after private statistic is modified then code using that classes have to be recompiled. Regularly this complaint is expressed as "abstract types in C++ aren't really abstract." What Bjarne Stroustrup hadn't found out was that many human beings idea that because they could put the illustration of an object within the private section of a class announcement then they virtually had to placed it there. This is actually incorrect (and that there was hassle for years).

If you do not need a representation in a class, accordingly, making the magnificence an interface only, you then really postpone the specification of the representation to some derived magnificence and outline simplest digital functions. For example, one can define a setof T pointers like this:

```
Class set { public :
Virtual        void
insert(T*); virtual
void remove(T*) ;
Virtual         int
is_member(T*);
V
i
r
t
u
a
l
T
*
f
i
r
s
t
(
)
;
V
i
```

```
rtual T* next();
Virtual-set(){}
};
```

This provides all the information that people need to use a set, except that whoever actuallymade a set must know something about how a few particular kind of set is represented
For example, given

```
Class slist_set : public set,
private slist { slink*
current_elem;Public:
Void insert(T*);
Void
remove(
T*); int is
member
(T*);
Virtual
T* first();
virtual
T*
next();
Slist_set(
) : slist(),
current_
elem(0) {
});
```

We can create slist_set gadgets that may be used as sets through users who've in no way heard of a
Slist_set. The handiest problem become that in C++, as defined earlier than 2.0, there has been no express manner of pronouncing: "The set class is just an interface: its functions neednot be defined, it is an error to create objects of class set,

and each person who derives a category from set must outline the virtual features specified in set." release 2.0 allowed a category to be declared explicitly abstract via declaring one or more of its virtual capabilities"natural" using the syntax = 0:

Class set { // abstract class public :
Virtual void insert(T*) = 0; // pure virtual function virtual void remove(T*) = 0;
// ..o);

The =0 syntax is not exactly wonderful; however, it expresses the preferred perception of a natural virtual characteristic in a way that is terse and fits the use of 0 to mean "not anything"or "no longer there" in C and C++. The opportunity, introducing a new keyword, say natural, wasn't a choice. Given the opposition to abstract classes as a "late and unimportant

exchange," Bjarne Stroustrup had in no way simultaneously have triumph over the traditional, strong, full-size, and emotional competition to new key phrases in components of the C and C++ community.

The significance of the abstract class idea is that it allows a cleaner separation among a user and an implementor than is viable without it. This limits the amount of recompilation vital after an alternate and also the quantity of records important to compile a median piece of code. Via reducing the coupling between a consumer and an implementor, abstraction classes provided a solution to user complaining about lengthy compile duration, and also serve libraryproviders who need to worry approximately the effect on users of adjustments to a library implementation.

4.5 Libraries

The first actual code written in C with instructions was the task library [Stroustrup 1980b], which supplied Simula like concurrency for simulation. The first real packages have been simulations of community site visitors, circuit board layout, and so forth, the use of the project library. The project library continues to be heavily used today. The usual C library changed into available from C++, without overhead or worry in comparison with C, from day one. So are all different C libraries. Classical data types, along with character strings, range checked arrays, dynamic arrays, and lists, have been a few of the examples used to design C++ and check its early implementations.

The early work with field classes such as list and array were significantly hampered through the shortage of assist for a manner of expressing parameterized types in C with classes and inC++ up until version 3.0. In the absence of proper language assist later supplied within the shape of templates, we needed to make do with macros. The first-rate that can be said for the C preprocessor's macro centers is that they allowed us to advantage enjoy with parameterized types and support individual and small organization use.

Much of the work on designing classes become finished in cooperation with JonathanShopiro, who in 1983 produced list and string training that noticed extensive use inside AT&Tand are the idea for the instructions currently determined inside the "general additives" library that turned into advanced in ring labs, and is now offered by using USL. The design ofthose early libraries interacted at once with the design of the language and especially with the design of the overloading mechanisms.

4.6 Compilers

The Santa Fe conference marked the announcement of the second one wave of C++ implementations. Steve Dewhurst defined the architecture of a compiler he and others had been building in AT&T's Summit facility, Mike Ball presented some thoughts for what have become the taumetric C++ compiler (greater regularly called the Oregon software program C++ compiler), and Mike Tiemann gave a maximum animated and exciting presentation of ways the GNU C++ he become building might do just about the whole thing and put all different C++ compiler writers out of commercial enterprise. The brand-new AT&T C++compiler by no means materialized; GNU C++ model 1.13 became first launched in Decemberof 1987; and taumetric C++ turned into first shipped in January of 1988.

Till June of 1988, all C++ compiler on computers were Cfront ports. Then Zortech started transport their compiler. The advent of Walter vivid's compiler made C++ "actual" for plenty computer-orientated people for the primary time. Greater conservative human beings reserved their judgment until the Borland C++ compiler in can also of 1990, or maybe Microsoft's C++ compiler in March 1992. DEC launched their first independently advanced C++ compiler in February of 1992 and IBM released their first independently advanced C++ compiler in May of 1992. In all, there are actually extra than a dozen independently evolved C++ compilers.

Similarly, to these compilers, Cfront ports regarded to be everywhere. Specially, sun, HP, Centerline, parcplace, Glockenspiel, and Comeau Computing ship Cfront-based totally products on just about any platform.

4.7 Tools and Environments

C++ was designed to be a possible language in a tool-poor environment. This was partly a need due to the almost complete lack of sources within the early years and the relative poverty in a while. It changed into additionally an aware decision to permit easy implementations and, mainly, easy porting of implementations.

C++ programming environments at the moment are emerging that are a suit for the environments habitually supplied with different object-oriented languages. For example, object works for C++ from parcplace is essentially the great Smalltalk program improvement surroundings tailored for C++, and Centerline C++ (formerly Saber C++) is an interpreter-based totally C++ surroundings, inspired by means of the interlisp environment. This gives C++ programmers the option of using the whizzier, extra expensive, and frequently greater productive environments that have previously handiest been available for different languagesand/or as research toys.

An environment is a framework in which tools can cooperate. There may be now a number of such environments for C++: most C++ implementations on pcs are compilers embedded ina framework of editors, equipment, document systems, standard libraries, and so on. Macappand the Mac MPW is the Apple Mac model of that and ET++ is a public area model within thestyle of the macapp. Eucid's Energize and HP's Softbench are yet different examples.

4.8 Minor Features

The ARM supplied some minor functions that had been not applied until 2.1 releases from AT&T and different C++ compiler carriers. The most obvious of these have been nested classes. Bjarne Stroustrup strongly recommended to revert to the original definition of nested class scopes by comments from external reviewers of the reference guide. Bjarne Stroustrup additionally despaired of ever getting the scope policies of C++ coherent even as the C rule turned into in vicinity.

The ARM allowed users to overload prefix and postfix increment (++) independently. The principle impetus for that got here from those who desired "smart pointers" that behaved exactly like normal recommendations except for some brought work performed "behind thescenes."

4.9 Templates

Within the original design of C++, parameterized types (templates) have been taken into consideration but postponed because there wasn't time to do a thorough activity of exploring the design and implementation troubles. Bjarne Stroustrup first presented templates at the 1988 USENIX C++ conference in Denver:

For plenty of people, the biggest alone trouble using C++ is the shortage of an extensive standard library. A chief hassle in producing any such library is that C++ does now not offer a sufficiently popular facility for defining "container training" together with lists, vectors, and associative arrays. [Stroustrup 1988b]

There are two approaches for supplying such classes/types: one can rely on dynamic typing and inheritance, as Smalltalk does, or one can rely upon static typing and a facility for arguments of kind type. The previous could be very flexible, however carries a high run-timecost, and more importantly, defies tries to use static type checking to seize interface errors.

Consequently, the latter technique turned into chosen.

A C++ parameterized kind is known as a category template. A class template specifies how character training can be constructed much like the way a class specifies how man or individual gadgets can be constructed. A vector class template is probably declared like this:

Template<class T> class vector
{
T
*
v
;
I
n
t
s
z
;
P
u
b
l
i
c
:
Vector(int);
T
&
o
p

e

r

a

t

o

r

[

]

(

i

n

t

)

;

T

&

e

l

e

m

(

i

n

t

i

)

{return v[i];) // ...

};

The template <class T> prefix specifies that a template is being declared and that an issue T of type *type* can be used inside the declaration. After its advent, T is used precisely like othertype names within the scope of the template assertion. Vectos can then be used like this:

```
Vector<int> vl(20); Vector<comple
```

```
x
>
v
2
(
3
0
)
;
```

Typedef vector<complex> cvec; // make cvec a synonym for // vector<complex>Cvec v3(40); // v2 and v3 are of the same type vl[3] = 7; V213] = v3. Elem(4) = complex(7,8) ;

C++ does no longer require the user to explicitly "instantiate" a template; that is, the user want not to specify which variations of a template need to be generated for precise units of template arguments. The motive is that most effective while the program is entire can it be acknowledged what templates need to be instantiated. Many templates might be defined in libraries and lots of instantiations may be without delay and in a roundabout way resulting from customers that don't even understand of the life of those templates. It therefore seemed unreasonable to require the consumer to request instantiations (say, via the use of something like Ada's 'new' operator).

Warding off useless space overheads because of too many instantiations of template functions become considered a primary order, that is, language level hassle instead of an implementation detail. I considered it not going that early (or even past due) implementations would be able to study instantiations of a class for unique template arguments and deduce that everyone or part of the instantiated code could be shared. The solution to this trouble changed into to use the derived class mechanism to make sure code sharing amongst derivedtemplate times.

The template mechanism is absolutely a compile and link time mechanism. No part of the template mechanism needs run-time guide. This leaves the hassle of the way to get the classes and capabilities generated (instantiated) from templates to depend on statistics recognized simplest at run time. The answer turned into, as ever in C++, to apply virtual functions and abstract instructions. Abstract classes used in reference to templates additionally have the effect of presenting better records hiding and higher separation of programs into independently compiled units.

4.10 ANSI and ISO

The initiative to formal (ANSI) standardization of C++ became taken by means of HP at the side of AT&T, DEC, and IBM. Larry Rosler from HP become critical on this initiative. The idea for ANSI standardization turned into written by using Dmitry Lenkov [Lenkov 1989]. Dmitry'sidea cites several reasons for fast standardization of C++:

• C++ is going via a much faster public recognition than most other languages.
• postpone will cause dialects.
• requires a cautious and specific definition imparting full semantics for every languagecharacteristic.

- C++ lacks some crucial functions ... Exception handling, factors of more than oneinheritance, capabilities helping parametric polymorphism, and preferred libraries.

The idea also burdened the want for compatibility with ANSI C. The organizational assembly of the ANSI C++ committee, X3J16, took place in December of 1989 in Washington, D.C. and was attended by means of about forty humans, inclusive of people who took component within the C standardization, individuals who with the aid of now have been "vintage time C++ programmers." Dmitry Lenkov have become its chairman and Jonathan Shopiro have become its editor.

The committee now has more than 250 individuals out of which something like 70 turn up atconferences. The purpose of the committee turned into, and is, a draft widespread for public overview in overdue 1993 or early 1994 with the wish of an official fashionable about two years later. Five that is an ambitious agenda for the standardization of a trendy-cause programming language. To compare, the standardization of C took seven years.

Naturally, standardization of C++ is not simply an American difficulty. From the start, representatives from other nations attended the ANSI C++ meetings; and in Lund, Sweden, inJune of 1991 the ISO C++ committee WG21 changed into convened and the 2 C++ requirements committees determined to maintain joint meetings--starting right now in Lund. Representatives from Canada, Denmark, France, Japan, Sweden, UK, and America have been gift. Substantially, the enormous majority of those country wide representatives were truly long-time C++ programmers. The C++ committee had a tough constitution:

1. The definition of the language need to be unique and comprehensive.
2. C/C++ compatibility needed to be addressed.
3. Extensions past modern-day C++ practice needed to be considered.
4. Libraries had to be taken into consideration.

On top of that, the C++ network was very diverse and definitely unorganized so that the standards committee clearly became an essential focal point of that community. In the quickrun, that is in reality the most important role for the committee.

C compatibility changed into the primary essential debatable issue we needed to face. After some time once in a while heated debate changed into decided that 100 percentage C/C++ compatibility wasn't an option. Neither become extensively reducing C compatibility. C++ was a separate language and no longer a strict superset of ANSI C and couldn't be changed to be this type of superset without breaking the C++ type machine and without breaking millions ofstrains of C++ code. This selection, often referred to as "As close to C, but no nearer" after a paper written by using Andrew Koenig and me [Koenig 1989a], is the equal that has been reached over and over again by individuals and organizations thinking about C++ and the pathof its evolution.

4.11 Retrospective

It is frequently claimed that hindsight is an actual technological know-how. It isn't. The claim is based totally at the false assumptions that we realize all relevant facts about what befell inside the past, that we realize the present-day scenario, and that we have a certainly detached point of view from which to choose the beyond. Usually none of those conditions maintain. This makes a retrospective on something as big, complicated, and dynamic as a programming language in large scale use unsafe.

1. Did C++ be successful at what it changed into designed for?
2. Is C++ a coherent language?
3. What turned into the most important mistake?

Evidently, the replies to these questions are related. The simple solutions are, 'yes,' 'sure,' and 'no longer delivery a bigger library with release 1.0'

4.12 Hopes for the Future

May C++ serve its purpose in community nicely. For that to happen, the language itself shouldbe strong and well specified. The C++ requirements group and the C++ compiler vendors have excellent responsibility here.
Similarly, to the language itself, we need libraries. Absolutely, we need a libraries industry toproduce, distribute, preserve, and teach people. This is emerging. The undertaking is to allow

packages to be composed out of libraries from specific vendors. This is hard and can want a few supports from the requirements committee within the form of popular instructions and mechanisms that ease the use of independently evolved libraries.

The language itself, plus the libraries, outline the language that a user de facto writes in. But,only through suitable information of the application regions and design strategies will the language and library features be positioned to correct use. Therefore, there need to be an emphasis on teaching people powerful design techniques and correct programming practices. The various strategies we need have still to be evolved, and most of the satisfactory techniques we do have nonetheless compete with simple lack of information and snake oil. Hope for a long way higher textbook for the C++ language and for programming and design techniques, and specifically for textbooks that emphasize the relationship between language features, accurate programming practices, and exact design techniques.

Techniques, languages, and libraries should be supported by equipment. The days of C++ programming supported with the aid of sincerely a "bare" compiler are nearly over, and the pleasant C++ equipment and environments are beginning to approach the energy and convenience of the nice tools and environments for any language. We will do tons better. Thebest has to come yet, hopefully.

Chapter 5

5.1 Uses of C++

There are numerous benefits of using C++ for developing programs and many applications product based developed in this language only because of its capabilities and safety. Please discover the underneath sections, where makes use of C++ has been widely and efficiently used.

```
        copy_from_user(group_info->blocks[i], grouplist, len))
            return -EFAULT;

        grouplist += NGROUPS_PER_BLOCK;
        count -= cp_count;
    }
    return 0;
}

/* a simple Shell sort */
static void groups_sort(struct group_info *group_info)
{
    int base, max, stride;
```

Below is the listing of the top uses of C++.

- **Applications:** its miles used for the development of new packages of C++. The applications based on the graphic person interface, which are exceedingly used programs like adobe photoshop and others. Many packages of Adobe systems are advanced in C++ likeIllustrator, adobe most advantageous and image geared up and Adobe builders areconsidered as energetic inside the C++ network.
- **Games:** This language is likewise used for developing games. It overrides the complexity of 3D video games. It allows in optimizing the sources. It helps the multiplayer alternative with networking. Makes use of C++ lets in procedural programming for extensive functions of CPU and to offer manage over hardware, and this language is very fast because of which it's far widely utilized in growing specific games or in gaming engines. C++ specially utilized in developing the suites of a sport device.
- **Animation:** there is animated software program, that's evolved with the assist of the C++language. 3D animation, modeling, simulation, rendering software program are referred to as the effective toolset. It's miles broadly used in building real-time, picture processing,cell sensor packages, and visible consequences, modeling which is particularly coded in C++. This evolved software used for animation, environments, motion pix, digital fact, and character creation. Virtual real devices are the maximum popular in these day's amusement international.
- **Web Browser:** This language is used for growing browsers as

nicely. C++ is used for makingGoogle Chrome, and Mozilla internet browser Firefox. A number of the applications are written in C++, from which Chrome browser is one among them and others are like a record machine, the map reduces huge cluster facts processing. Mozilla has other utility additionally written in C++ that is e-mail customer Mozilla Thunderbird. C++ is likewise a rendering engine for the open-source tasks of Google and Mozilla.

- **Database get admission to:** This language is likewise used for developing databasesoftware or open-source database software. The instance for that is mysql, which is one of the most famous database control software and widely utilized in corporations or the various developers. It allows in saving time, cash, commercial enterprise structures, and packaged software. There is different database software get admission to primarily based programs used which can be Wikipedia, Yahoo, youtube, etc. The alternative instance is Bloomberg RDBMS, which facilitates in presenting actual-time economic records to traders. It is in particular written in C++, which makes database get admission to fast and brief or accurate to deliver information concerning commercial enterprise and finance, information round the arena.

- **Compilers:** maximum of the compilers particularly written in C++ language most effective. The compilers which might be used for compiling different languages like C#, Java, and so on. Mainly written in C++ only. It is also used in developing those languages as well as C++ is platform-impartial and able to create a diffusion of software.

- **Running systems:** It's also used for growing most of the working structures for Microsoft and few elements of the Apple operating machine. Microsoft windows 95, ninety-eight, 2000, XP, workplace, net Explorer and visible studio, Symbian cell working systems are mainly written in C++ language only.

- **Scanning:** The packages like film scanner or digital camera scanner are also developed in the C++ language. It's been used for developing PDF era for print documentation, replacing documents, archiving the document and post the files as properly.

Conclusion

C++ is the language that is used anywhere however in particular in systems programming and embedded structures. Here system programming way for developing the running structures or drivers that interface with hardware. Embedded system method matters that are cars, robotics, and appliances. It is having a higher or wealthy network and developers, which helps in the smooth hiring of builders and on line solutions without difficulty. Uses of C++ is known as the safest language due to its security and functions. It is the primary language for any developer to start, who is inquisitive about operating in programming languages. It is straightforward to analyze, as it's far natural idea-based language. Its syntax is quite simple, which makes it clean to write down or develop and mistakes may be effortlessly replicated. Before the use of any other language, programmers preferred to analyze C++ first and then they used different languages. However maximum of the developers try to stay with C++ handiest due to its huge sort of usage and compatibility with more than one structures and software.

PYTHON CODING

AN INTRODUCTION TO NEURAL NETWORKS AND A BRIEF OVERVIEW OF THE PROCESSES YOU NEED TO KNOW WHEN PROGRAMMING COMPUTERS AND CODING WITH PYTHON

[Tony Coding]

Legal & Disclaimer

The information contained in this book and its contents is not designed to replace or take the place of any form of medical or professional advice; and is not meant to replace the need for independent medical, financial, legal or other professional advice or services, as may be required. The content and information in this book has been provided for educational and entertainment purposes only.

The content and information contained in this book has been compiled from sources deemed reliable, and it is accurate to the best of the Author's knowledge, information and belief. However, the Author cannot guarantee its accuracy and validity and cannot be held liable for any errors and/or omissions. Further, changes are periodically made to this book as and when needed. Where appropriate and/or necessary, you must consult a professional (including but not limited to your doctor, attorney, financial advisor or such other professional advisor) before using any of the suggested remedies, techniques, or information in this book.

Upon using the contents and information contained in this book, you agree to hold harmless the Author from and against any damages, costs, and expenses, including any legal fees potentially resulting from the application of any of the information provided by this book. This disclaimer applies to any loss, damages or injury caused by the use and application, whether directly or indirectly, of any advice or information presented, whether for breach of contract, tort, negligence, personal injury, criminal intent, or under any other cause of action.

You agree to accept all risks of using the information presented inside this book.

You agree that by continuing to read this book, where appropriate and/or necessary, you shall consult a professional (including but not limited to your doctor, attorney, or financial advisor or such other advisor as needed) before using any of the suggested remedies, techniques, or information in this book.

Introduction

Machine learning is permeating numerous aspects of our everyday lives, right from optimizing Netflix recommendations to Google searches. Machine learning has contributed to improving different facets of building mechanics in smart building space and the experiences of the occupant. You do not have to have a Ph.D. to understand the different facets and functions of machine learning. This section covers some facts about machine learning that are very basic and important to know.

Bifurcation of Machine Learning

Supervised and unsupervised machine learning are two techniques that programmers and scientists use to help machines learn. Smart buildings incorporate both types. Here is a simple example of how these types of machine learning look like: Let us assume that you want to teach a computer to recognize an ant. When you use a supervised approach, you will tell the computer that an ant is an insect that could either be small or big. You will also need to tell the computer that the ant could either be red or black. When you use an unsupervised approach, you will need to show the computer different animal groups and then tell the computer what an ant looks like and then show the computer another set of pictures and ask the computer to identify the ant until the computer learns the features specific to an ant.

Smart building spaces use both supervised and unsupervised machine learning techniques. The applications in these smart buildings allow the users to provide feedback to the building to improve the efficiency of the building.

Machines are not fully automatic

Machine learning helps computers automate, anticipate and evolve but that does not mean that they can take over the world. Machine learning uses algorithms that human beings develop. Therefore, machine learning still needs human beings since they will need to set parameters and train the machine with different training datasets.

Machine learning helps a computer discover patterns that are not possible for human beings to see. The computer will then make an adjustment to the system. However, it is not good to identify and understand why those patterns exist. For instance, smart buildings human beings created smart buildings to ensure that the people inside the building help to improve the living conditions of the people. However, one cannot expect that a machine will learn to become more productive. A human must set up the definitions and rules that the building will need to follow.

Anyone can use machine learning

Writing a machine learning algorithm is very different

from learning how to use that algorithm. After all, you do not need to learn how to program when you use an app on your phone. The best platforms always create an abstract of the program to present the users with an interface, which need minimal training to use. If you do know the basic concepts of machine learning, you are ready to go! Data scientists must edit or change the algorithms.

Machine learning has come of this age and is growing quickly. Buildings are using machine learning in different ways to make the existing infrastructure efficient and help to enhance the experience of the occupants residing in the building. Right from an energy usage standpoint, buildings are always learning and analyzing the needs of the occupants.

How does this affect us going forward? This advance in machine learning goes to say that most things will happen without the need for us to ask. Machine learning engineering could go beyond managing lighting and temperature. Machine learning implies that there will be some future state of multiple layers and levels of automation adjusting based on the current activity.

Data Transformation is where the work lies

When you read through the different techniques of machine learning, you will probably assume that machine learning is mostly about selecting the right algorithm and tuning that algorithm to function accurately. The reality is prosaic – a large chunk of your time goes into cleansing the data and then transforming that data into raw features that will define the relationship between your data.

Revolution of Machine Learning has begun

During the 1980s there was a rapid development and advancement in computing power and computers. This gave rise to enormous amount of fear and excitement around artificial intelligence, computers and machine learning which could help the world solves a variety of ailments – right from household drudgery to diseases. As artificial intelligence and machine learning developed as formal fields of study, turning these ideas and hopes into reality was more difficult to achieve and artificial intelligence retreated into the world of theory and fantasy. However, in the last decade, the advances in data storage and computing have changed the game again. Machines are now able to work on tasks that once were difficult for them to learn.

Chapter 1:An introduction to python machine learning

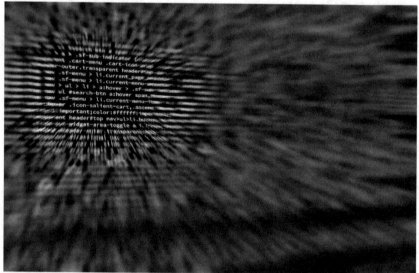

Machine learning is both the application and the science of algorithms that can make some sense out of data. It is an incredibly exciting part of the computer sciences arena and, like it or not, it's here to stay. The world today is full of data and using algorithms that have the capacity to learn. This means that this data can be used to create knowledge. In the last few years, there have been quite a few open-source libraries developed, some of them incredibly powerful, and that means we are probably at the peak time to start truly understanding machine learning, to start learning how to use these algorithms to find data patterns and predict future events.

Do you remember when you got your first computer? For most people, the device was so foreign to them they couldn't even understand what they were supposed to do with it. No doubt, for many people, they still wanted one even if they had no idea what its true purpose was. Even today, there are numerous people who have found computers nothing more than a great device for playing games, binge-watching their favorite TV shows, or streaming their favorite music.

But you can do so many amazing things if you know how to tap into the true potential of these wonderful devices. Once a person knows what to do with modern day machines, things begin to change in very big ways. We can easily take a task and go beyond the basics. When that happens, computers become far more than a glorified calculator that can decipher calculations and numbers in a fraction of a second. To get to that point there are a few things that you must understand.

Machines now do not need to have every detail of their functions automatically programmed. They can be programmed to learn a number of tasks and make the necessary adjustments to perform the functions that will allow them to work more efficiently.

Frankly, there are certain computer functions that many assume to be advanced technology but are merely things that can be done very quickly. For example, at the heart of every computer is a very complex calculator. When the computer performs an action we think is fascinating, it is merely the machine performing a number of mathematical equations to produce the results we desire.

You might want to stream your favorite movie to your computer. You click a few buttons and in a matter of seconds, scenes begin to play out in front of your eyes. Really, this function is nothing more than the computer running a bunch of basic math problems in the background, taking the sums and reconstructing them into a video on your screen.

This may seem like science fiction but the possibility is all too real, thanks to the creation of neural networks. In its simplest of terms, neural networks are a series of mathematical formulas called algorithms that identify relationships in a group of data. The network can accomplish this by mimicking the human brain and how it works.

These are complicated networks that are capable of adapting to constantly changing data so that it can achieve the best results possible without having to redesign the criteria needed to get the optimum output.

To put it more simply, neural networks are the means of injecting flexibility into a computer system so that it processes data in a way that is similar to how the human brain works. Of course, computers are still going to be made in the same way as other machines but with each improvement, they are getting closer and closer to thinking machines rather than devices that are strictly following a static set of instructions.

Before we can fully understand neural networks, we have to get a firm grasp on what we mean when we talk about a machine that can learn. We are not talking about giving machines textbooks, homework, and exams so they can learn in the same way a student does. That would be ridiculous, but it helps to see just how a computer can mimic the human brain. So, let's look at how the human brain works first and make a comparison.

When a human being absorbs new information, they usually gain the information from something they're not familiar with. It could come in the form of a question or a statement of something new, or it could come as an experience with no verbal connection whatsoever. The information is picked up through the body's five senses and transmitted directly to the brain. The brain then reshuffles a number of its neural pathways (we call this thinking) so it can process the information and then when all the details related to the information is compared and analyzed in the brain, an answer or a conclusion is drawn and instructions are sent out to the rest of the body.

Since computers don't really think, they have to accomplish the same goal but in a different way. Information is inputted into the computer's programming, it is then processed, calculated, and analyzed based on a number of preset algorithms, and then a conclusion, prediction, or answer is drawn and it comes out as output.

Let's look at an example. Let's say you want to figure out the answer to the problem 9 - 8. This is a basic math question that will require you to 'think' in order to get the right answer. While we will do this very quickly, we need to understand what is happening in our brain so we can see the similarity with computers.

When we receive information, our senses automatically send all the data relating to it to the brain. The brain is made up of billions of neurons that are all interconnected, creating miles upon miles of pathways where information can travel. What's really neat about our brain is that these pathways are constantly shifting based on the data that is being transmitted. When new information is received, they will shift to create new pathways to transmit it to where it needs to go in the brain. Throughout this process, this shifting will continue until a solution is decided upon. Then instructions are sent throughout the body's central nervous system to different parts of the body instructing them on the proper way to respond to the information received. The brain accomplishes all of this in fractions of a second.

In a neural network, the same thing happens. While these networks cannot perfectly mimic the inner workings of the brain, the process is very similar. The information is taken in and the neural network does all the work of consuming data, processing it, and coming up with a workable solution. These networks allow the computer to 'learn' by using algorithms.

Turning Data into Knowledge

We live in a modern world filled with technology. Every day, we hear that the planet is being stripped of its resources but there is one resource that continues to grow, a resource that we have plenty of – data, both structured and unstructured. In the last 50 years of the 20th century, machine learning began to evolve. It was an AI subfield that used algorithms that could learn; algorithms that could derive knowledge from the data and use this knowledge to make predictions for the future. Where once a human being would have been needed to manually make the rules and build the models by analyzing vast amounts of data, machine learning does it much quicker and more efficiently. Machine learning allows us to capture the data, turn it into knowledge, and make improvements to how predictive modeling performed; the result of this is decisions driven by data.

So, you can see how important machine learning is in terms of computer sciences research, but do you realize just how often it features in everyday life? Think about the strong spam filters on your email, voice recognition on your computers and mobile devices, convenient text, decent search engines on the web, computerized Chess games and, in the future, safe self-drive cars. All of this is thanks to the advances made in machine learning.

Algorithms

No doubt, you've heard the term before. It is often associated with all sorts of technical mechanics but in recent years algorithms are being used in the development of automatic learning, the field that is leading us to advancements in artificial and computational intelligence. This is a method of analyzing data in a way that makes it possible for machines to analyze and process data. With this type of data, computers can work out and perform a number of tasks it could not originally do. They can understand different concepts, make choices, and predict possibilities for the future.

To do this, the algorithms have to be flexible enough to adapt and make adjustments when new data is presented. They are therefore able to give the needed solution without having to create a specific code to solve a problem. Instead of programming a rigid code into the system, the relevant data becomes part of the algorithm which in turn, allows the machine to create its own reasoning based on the data provided.

How does this work?

This might sound a little confusing but we'll try to break this down into certain examples you can relate to. One of the 'learning' functions of machines is the ability to classify information. To do this, the input data can be a mix of all types of information. The algorithm needs to identify the different elements of the data and then group them into several different categories based on characteristics of similarities, differences, and other factors.

These characteristics can be any number of things ranging from identifying handwriting samples to the types of documents received. If this were code, the machine could only do one single function but because it is an algorithm which can be altered to fit a wide variety of things, the computer can receive this data and classify all sorts of groups that fit within the specific parameters of the circumstances.

This is how machines can change their functions to adapt to the situation at hand. Your email account can analyze all the emails you received, based on a pattern that you have followed, and it divides them into different groups. It can identify which emails are important and you should see right away, those that are spam and junk mail, and even sort out those that may pose a risk to your computer because it carries a virus or malware.

With these types of algorithms, machines can now learn by observing your habits and patterns and adjust their behavior accordingly. So, the very secret to a successful and effective neural pathway depends a great deal on the algorithms your system uses.

Three Types of Machine Learning

Without algorithms, machines cannot learn. So, over the years many different ones have been developed. In this part of the chapter, we will look in detail at the three machine learning types. They are:

- Supervised learning

- Unsupervised learning

- Reinforcement Learning

We'll describe the basic differences between the three and explain the practicalities of applying the principles.

Supervised Learning – Predicting the Future

A supervised algorithm requires a detailed input of related data over a period of time. Once all the information is available to the computer, it is used to classify any new data relating to it. The computer then does a series of calculations, comparisons, and analysis before it makes a decision.

This type of algorithm requires an extensive amount of information to be programmed into the system so that the computer can make the right decision. That way, when it needs to solve a problem, it will attempt to determine which mathematical function it needs to use in order to find the correct solution. With the right series of algorithms already programmed into the system, the machine can sift through all types of data in order to find the solution to a wide variety of problems in the related category.

Supervised algorithms are referred that way because they require human input to ensure that the computer has the right data to process the information it receives.

Supervised learning has one basic goal – to learn a specified model from "labeled" data for training purposes so that predictions can be made about future data or unseen data. It is called "supervised" because the labels, or the output signals that we want, are known already.

Think about your email, about the spam filter in place. We could use supervised machine learning to train a model. The data would be labeled – emails already marked correctly as spam, those marked correctly as not spam – and the model would be trained to recognize to which group new emails belong. When you have supervised tasks such as this, using class labels, we call it a "classification task".

Predicting Class Labels Using Classification

So, classification is a subcategory with a goal of predicting under which class label new instances would be placed. This is based on previous data. The labels are discrete with values in no order that can be understood to be memberships of the instances. The example of spam filters is representative of a binary type of classification task – the algorithm will learn the rules so that it can work out the difference between potential classes – spam and not spam.

Although this is a binary classification task, the class labels are not required to be binary in nature. The learning algorithm will determine a predictive model that can then assign any of the labels from the dataset to a new instance that has no label. One example of this type of multiclass classification is the recognition of handwritten characters. We could have a dataset that has the letters of the alphabet written in several different handwriting styles. If the user were to use an input device to give a new character, the predictive model could predict which letter of the alphabet it was with accuracy. However, the system could not recognize any digit from 0 to 9 because they would not be in the dataset used for training purposes.

Let's say that we have 30 pieces of sample data – 15 of

them are labeled as a positive class with a plus sign (+) and 15 are labeled as a negative class with a minus sign (-). The dataset is called a two-dimensional dataset, meaning that each of the samples has two possible values, x1 and x2. Supervised learning algorithms could be used to learn the rule that a dashed line is used to represent the decision boundary and this rule is used to separate the classes and put any new data into one of the categories depending on the x1 and x2 values.

Continuous Outcome Prediction Using Regression

We know now that classification tasks are used for assigning unordered, categorical labels to instances. There is another type of supervised learning called regression analysis, and this is used for the prediction of continuous outcomes. With regression analysis, we have several explanatory or predictor variables, along with a variable for a continuous response. We can predict outcomes by finding relationships between the variables. Let me give an example. We have a class of students and we want to try to predict their SAT scores. If we can find a link between how long each student studied and their scores, we could then use that data to learn models that can use the length of time studied to predict the score achieved by future students.

Reinforcement Learning – Solving Interactive Problems

Reinforcement Learning is another area of machine learning and the goal here is to develop an agent or system that can improve its performance. This improvement is based on how the agent interacts with its environment. Information that details the current environmental state tends to include a reward-signal, so this kind of machine learning can be considered a part of supervised learning. However, the feedback in Reinforcement Learning is not the right value or truth label; rather, it is an indication of how the reward function related to the action. By interacting with its environment, the agent learns several actions to maximize the reward. By using Reinforcement Learning, the agent will go through an approach of either deliberate planning or trial and error to get the reward.

Reinforcement learning is commonly used in video games where the computer must navigate and adjust its movements in order to win the game. A reward system is used so the computer knows and understands when it should make the right move, but there are also negative consequences whenever they make errors. This type of algorithm works best in situations where the computer has an obstacle that it must overcome like a rival in a game, or it could also be a self-driving car that needs to reach its destination. The entire focus of the computer is to accomplish certain tasks while navigating the unpredictable environment around it. With each mistake, the computer will readjust its moves in order to reduce the number of errors so it can achieve the desired result.

A Chess engine is a great example of this type of machine learning. The agent will decide on the moves it will make, dependent on the environment (the board) and the reward is defined as winning or losing when the game is over.

Reinforcement Learning has a number of subtypes but, in general, the agent will carry out several environmental interactions in an attempt to get the maximum reward. Each of the states is associated with a negative or a positive reward – the reward is defined by achieving a specific goal, in this case, losing or winning the game of Chess. For example, in a game of Chess, the outcome of a move is a state of that environment.

Let's go a bit deeper into this. Take the locations of each square on the Chessboard. Visiting them could be given a positive reward association – you take an opponent's piece or put his king or queen under threat, for example. Other locations have a negative reward association – losing one of your pieces by having your own king or queen put under threat in the next turn. Not every game turn will end with a piece being removed from the board so where does Reinforcement Learning come into this? Quite simply, it is about learning the series of steps that are needed by ensuring the maximum reward based on feedback – immediate and delayed.

This really is as far as we can go on Reinforcement Learning. We can only give you a basic overview because applications for this type of learning are way beyond the scope of this guide which is focusing on clustering, classification, and regression analysis.

Unsupervised Learning – Discovering Hidden Structures

With supervised learning, we already know the answer we want when the model is being trained. With Reinforcement Learning, we provide a reward measured by specific actions performed by the agent. With unsupervised learning, we are going one step further by using unlabeled data – data with unknown structure. By using these techniques, we can explore the data structure to get meaningful information without needing to be guided by a reward or by a variable with a known outcome.

An unsupervised algorithm implies that the computer does not have all the information to make a decision. Maybe it has some of the data needed but one or two factors may be missing. This is kind of like the algebra problems you encountered in school. You may have two factors in the problem but you must solve the third on your own. A + b = c. If you know A but you have no idea what b is then you need to plug the information into an equation to solve the problem.

With unsupervised learning, this can be an extremely complex type of problem to solve. For this type of problem, you'll need an algorithm that recognizes various elements of a problem and can incorporate that into the equation. Another type of algorithm will look for any inconsistencies in the data and try to solve the problem by analyzing those.

Unsupervised algorithms clearly are much more complex than the supervised algorithms. While they may start with some data to solve a problem, they do not have all the information so they must be equipped with the tools to find those missing elements without having a human to provide all the pieces of the puzzle for them.

Use Clustering to Find Subgroups

Clustering is a technique of exploratory data analysis which lets us organize a great amount of data into subgroups or clusters. We do not have any upfront knowledge about the group memberships. Each of the clusters identified from the analysis will define a specific group of objects that are similar to a certain degree but are not quite so similar to objects that are in the other clusters. This is why you often hear clustering being termed as "unsupervised classification". Clustering is absolutely one of the best techniques we have for providing a structure to a set of information and determining meaningful relationships from the information. For example, think of marketers. They can use clustering to determine specific customer groups by their interests so that they can devise a targeted marketing program.

Dimensionality Reduction

This is another subfield of the unsupervised machine learning area. More often than not, high-dimensionality data is used. This means that each observation has several measurements. This presents a bit of a challenge where storage space is limited and affects the performance of the learning algorithms. Dimensionality reduction, in terms of unsupervised machine learning, is used quite often in feature preprocessing, to remove the noise from the data. This noise can cause degradation in the predictive performance of some algorithms. It is also commonly used to compress data so it fits into a smaller subspace while keeping the relevant information intact. Occasionally, we can also use dimensionality reduction for visualizing data. For example, we could project a high-dimensionality feature set onto 1, 2, or 3D feature spaces – this would allow us to see that feature set through 2D or 3D histograms or scatterplots.

Semi-supervised learning

Semi-supervised learning is a blend of both supervised and reinforcement learning. The computer is given an incomplete set of data from which to work. Some of the data include specific examples of previous decisions made with the available data while other data is missing completely. These algorithms work on solving a specific problem or performing very specific functions that will help them achieve their goals.

Of course, these are not the only algorithms that can be used in a computer program to help the machine learning. But, the general idea is the same. The algorithm must fit with the problem the computer needs to solve.

Machine Learning Systems – Building a Roadmap

Up to this point, we have looked at the basic machine learning concepts and the different machine learning types. Now we need to look at the rest of a machine learning system, the important parts that go with the algorithm. There are three important subsections to consider.

Preprocessing

Preprocessing is the act of getting our data into shape. Raw data is very rarely in the right format or shape required for the learning algorithm to work properly.

The images of the flowers are the raw data from which we will be looking for meaningful features. Those features could be color, intensity, hue, height, length of the flower, width of the flower, and so on. A lot of machine learning algorithms will also require the chosen features to be on identical scales for the best performance and this is achieved by transforming features in a range or by using standard distribution with "zero mean and unit variance". Some of the features selected may be correlated and that means, to a certain extent, they are redundant. In these cases, we can use the dimensionality reduction to compress those features down to a lower subspace. By doing this, we don't need as much storage space and the algorithm is significantly faster. In some cases, reduction can also make the predictive model performance more efficient, especially if the dataset has got multiple instances of noise (features that are not relevant) – you will often see this as having a low ratio of signal to noise. To see if the algorithm is performing as it should on the training dataset while reacting positively to new data, we will need to divide the dataset randomly into two sets – training and test. The training dataset trains the model and optimizes performance, while the test set is used last to evaluate the finished model.

Training and Choosing Predictive Models

You will see throughout this guide that many of the algorithms are designed to solve specific problems. There is one important thing to remember – learning is not free. This concept can easily be related to another popular saying by Abraham Maslow in 1966 – "I suppose it is tempting, if the only tool you have is a hammer, to treat everything as if it were a nail". Let's put this into context. Every one of the classification algorithms has got biases built into it. No one classification model is superior to any other provided we make no assumptions regarding the task. In practical terms, it is vital that several algorithms are compared so that the best model can be selected and trained. However, before we can do this, we need to decide which metric we are using to measure the performance. One of the most common metrics is classification accuracy and this is defined as a set proportion of instances that have been classified correctly. But, and this is a legitimate question, how will we know which of the models will perform the best on the final test and on real-world data if the test set is used ONLY for the final evaluation and NOT on the model selection tests? To address this issue, we can use multiple techniques for cross-validation – the training dataset is split into two subsets: training and validation. This is done so that the model's generalization performance can be estimated. Lastly, although many software libraries offer learning algorithms, we should not take it for granted that the default parameters of these algorithms will fit the specific problem we are trying to solve. Instead, we will use techniques called hyperparameter optimization to fine-tune our model's performance and we'll see how this is done later. Basically, the hyperparameters can be thought of as parameters that cannot be learned from the dataset but instead, they represent dials that we can turn to improve the performance of the model.

Model Evaluation and Prediction of Unseen Data Instances

Once we have our model, the test dataset can be used to estimate how the model performs on unseen data. In this way, we can gain an estimation of the generalization error percentage. If we are happy with the way the model performs, we can use it for predicting future data. Be aware of one thing – it is vital that the parameters for the procedures we talked about, like dimensionality reduction and feature scaling, are obtained ONLY from the training dataset and are then applied to the test dataset to transform it. They are also applied to new samples of data. If we don't adhere to this, the test data may produce an overly-optimistic performance measurement.

Problems Of Machine Learning

Machine Learning is still evolving and still being used every day. As it is used more, the more we are going to be able to figure out where the problems are and what needs to be done to fix them. Some of these problems are yet to be solved, but that does not mean that there will not be a solution later in the future.

One problem is that natural language processing and understanding language is still a problem when it comes to Machine Learning, even with the deepest networks. Because of the many different languages and dialects, it is hard for machines to decipher what is being said. But that does not stop them from trying. Programs such as Alexa, Siri and Cortana are constantly being updated so that they can better serve their users.

Images can be classified with Machine Learning, but it cannot figure out what is going on in the image. By understanding what is going on in an image, it cannot be further classified. But we are going to have the option to figure out where the influences in the image lie and how we would be able to recreate the work in the same style. This also leads to solving semantic segmentation. Machines should be taught how to identify what is going on in each pixel so that we can better understand what is going on in the image.

Deep reinforcement needs to be stabilized as well. If something is not broken, why attempt to fix it? Sometimes the old ways work the best, and there is no reason to be messing with the model that already works. With deep reinforcement being stabilized, this would be possible. This is then going to allow deep reinforcement to tackle harder problems that have yet to be touched by Machine Learning such as Montezuma's revenge.

On top of that, with stabilized reinforcement, learning the ability to control robotics would open up exponentially, and the possibilities would be endless. There is no telling how far robotics would go because they would be able to figure out the best way to receive their reward; in other words, they would be given the option to act like humans but have an incentive as to what they should do to get that reward.

GANs are generative adversarial networks that are going to work with a specific class of artificial intelligence. It is a set of algorithms that will be used with unsupervised learning which will then be implemented on a system of two neural networks working against each other in a zero-sum game framework. While they are great for those who use Machine Learning for games, they are highly stabilized and make gaming harder because they are known to frequently crash.

Training deep nets is an issue as well because it has been proven by the shattering of gradients paper that those that use Machine Learning do not understand yet how to train their nets properly. That also leads to the fact that no one quite understands what deep nets do in general. There have been those that have written papers on what deep nets are and why they are required, but then there have been those that have written papers on how deep nets are not needed, and they tend to make life more complicated. So, why are deep nets there? And do we actually need them?

Lastly, there has to be a way to get people to stop worrying so much about things such as Skynet and the economic impact. First of all, Skynet is a fictional company in the movie Terminator and is not going to happen. Before robots are able to make their own decisions if ever, there will no doubt be a failsafe in place that is going to ensure that the robots do not rise up against humans and try to kill them. All Skynet is, is a good plot for a movie franchise that millions of people love. Secondly, what is the economic impact of Machine Learning? With Machine Learning, companies are going to have the ability to figure out where they are going to make more money and that means that more money is going to be put into the economy!

Besides certain things in Machine Learning not being stabilized, Machine Learning does not have that many problems. It is hard to remember that Machine Learning is still In its infancy and is still being trained as technology evolves, so we have to be patient and keep in mind that there are going to be more problems before they are to be fixed.

Problems with Machine Learning That Have Not Been Solved

Machine Learning is evolving as technology evolves, so it is highly likely that there are always going to be issues that will have to be dealt with before an answer is found. There are going to be ways around these issues, and even if there are not, there are going to be ways for you to analyze and get your data results despite these issues. Below, are a few issues that have yet to be solved by Machine Learning.

One, the variable event space has not been solved yet to solve this, we are going to need to be able to create a classification system that is going to respond in an efficient and meaningful way even if the event space is varying from the training data.

Another one is that there is no context understanding when it comes to the processing languages. Context analysis is a big deal for Machine Learning because it leaves a large hole open for things to be misunderstood.

One possible solution is that the open AI team should come up with a solution that allows the agents to create their own rules instead of making it to where they need to find patterns.

Facial identification is quickly becoming a popular way for people to unlock their device because it is quick and a semi-secure way to keep your device from being hacked. However, it is by no means perfect because people with similar facial features will be able to get into each other's phone. Not only that but if a female wears makeup and does not for the facial recognition picture, then she is not going to be able to get into her phone because she altered her appearance.

Automated learning is a big part of Machine Learning, and if a machine cannot automatically learn what it is supposed to, then it is not going to be useful to the company that is using it. Learning has to come from a variety of resources, and when a graph is being made based on the connected sense that is missing, then the automated learning is going to hit a snag and is going to have gaps in what it is able to do. For example, IBM's Watson has been doing an excellent job, but it still requires a system that is more geared toward automated general intelligence.

In some Machine Learning, the machine is going to need to make its own decisions based on its reasoning over a deviating test space; but this is not going to include the rule-based engines. To make the reasoning that is required, Machine Learning will need to have space for reasoning or debatable agents that will help with its reasoning.

Have you ever talked to Siri and she got confused if you are trying to talk to her or if you are talking to someone else? This is an issue that Machine Learning has with its efficient repose generation. In other words, Siri cannot create a contextual response when you are talking to her unless it is already programmed in or if she can look it up on the internet.

The three-way human rule is an issue with Machine Learning as well. Machines cannot always comprehend the knowledge that humanity has a three-way rule that takes an image, gives it a type, and then gives it a description. If Machine Learning could comprehend the three-way human rule, then classifying art, music, and others would be an easier task.

Another issue that Machine Learning has shown is its memory networks. Many people believe that working with technology means that you do not need a lot of space. However, this is far from true because to store all of the data that is collected, there needs to be a lot of space available.

Machines are not humans, so they are not going to be able to come up with the thoughts that a human is able to come up with. But machines can be taught as long as we do not push them past their limits, but we do not limit them to where all of the work still needs to be done by a human. Technology is going to have its hold-ups, but eventually, they can be solved. One reason they may not be solved yet is that the technology needed to solve it does not exist yet.

Problems That Can Be Solved

Machine Learning is helping out a lot of companies as well as individuals in their daily lives. In this section, you will see some points that were mentioned above as problems that have not been solved by Machine Learning just yet. Even though there are issues with that particular piece of Machine Learning, that does not mean that it does not work. Sometimes, these issues can be patched or fixed at a later date while the software is put out for users to use and discover what issues there may be with the software that the developers did not catch.

Machine Learning helps with spam detection. When you get into your inbox, there are always emails that automatically gets routed to your spam box because of keywords that are detected in other emails. Yet some spam is allowed through because these keywords have been found in your inbox. It is going to filter those keywords to your inbox on the slight chance that you are going to want the emails even though they are spam. Spam detection still has a long way to go, but it is getting better as more rules are made.

Have you ever wondered how the credit card companies are able to know when someone has used your card? It is because of the transaction record that they keep! Every month, the credit card company knows your usual stores and about how much is going to be spent. If they see any activity outside of your usual area or outside of how much you usually spend, they are going to say that the card was stolen and report it as such. This can cause problems later on if you decide to go on a trip or if you spend over what you normally spend.

It is not perfect, but Machine Learning is learning how to recognize zip codes written on envelopes so that they are able to sort the envelopes out into geographical locations and that way the mail is sorted faster and is delivered faster. There are still some issues with this as machines are not always able to read a person's handwriting since everyone writes in a different manner.

As mentioned, Siri or Cortana is able to understand what you are saying. But, what if other machines were also capable of doing this? Thanks to Machine Learning, this is now becoming a reality. The biggest issue is that everyone has different dialects and speaks a different language. Not only that, but new words are being added to the dictionary almost daily. But, even with there being issues in machine's understanding of what is being said to them, this does not stop them from trying to fulfill the request that is made.

When you upload a picture on Facebook, there is an algorithm that looks at the facial features of those in the picture and asks you if you would like to tag that person. This allows the person to see the picture where they were tagged and allows them to decide if they want it on their profile or not. The same algorithm is used when a user decides to use the facial recognition software on their phone or computer to unlock their device.

Everyone knows when they log into websites such as Amazon, there is a list of products that are recommended to you because of your past purchases or because of things that you have looked at. There is a model that is built-in to the code of the website that allows it to figure out ways to target you specifically as an individual so that you are given a more personalized shopping experience. In doing this, Amazon and other websites that use the same algorithm are hoping that they are going to be able to keep you coming back to spend money with them. This algorithm can also be seen in Facebook because it allows you to log into other websites so that it can provide you with ads that you may want to see instead of generic ads that are not going to catch your attention.

The medical field has to advance with technology, or else it falls behind. Because of Machine Learning, the medical field is able to take the symptoms that a patient is feeling. This allows them to plug the symptoms into their computer and get a list of diagnosis. This is not going to be perfect, but it is going to point the healthcare provider in the right direction so that they are able to figure out what is wrong with the patient.

When it comes to trading stock, it is vital to know when you are going to trade or hold on to your stock so can make more money. Machine Learning has come up with an algorithm that looks at the financial information and analyzes it so that stockbrokers are able to know when they should trade and when they should let their stocks go. This is helping many companies save money, so they are not buying useless stocks or so that they are not holding onto a stock that is about to lose all of its value.

Data entry by humans is going to have issues such as duplication and inaccurate data. But, with Machine Learning, algorithms work with predictive modeling algorithms to improve these issues. They learn how to perform time-intensive documentation and other data entry tasks. This opens up more free time for those with the proper knowledge to be able to work on the more intensive problem-solving tasks because they do not need to deal with the menial data entry jobs that machines are able to do.

Machine Learning is used by most of the companies that are in business today. It may not be used in a way that is automatically visible to the general public or even their employees, but it is being used even in the simple way of analyzing data. This aids them in making better decisions in gaining money rather than losing money.

Where And How Machine Learning Is Used

Machine learning is already in widespread use in many different industries. It's used for anti-lock braking, autopilot in airplanes, search engines, product recommendations, maps, and driving directions, spam screeners, language translation, personal digital assistants, weather maps, and more. Any organization that has a lot of data and is looking for better ways to understand and use that data can benefit from this technology.

Several companies have used machine learning to build some of the most lucrative businesses on a getting-to-know-you-better platform. Google, Facebook, Apple, LinkedIn, and Twitter are all using machine learning to make sure you have access to relevant data. Some companies are even pushing the envelope of privacy by analyzing your search history or personal or professional connections. By learning more about you they can personalize their service for you. That's why your Facebook newsfeed is completely unique to you. It's also why two people googling the exact same search term may get completely different results.

Any time you're on a website and you see something like "recommended for you," you're probably benefiting from machine learning. Amazon may examine your previous purchases and then use machine learning to recommend other products you might like. Netflix tries to figure out your taste in movies to suggest other shows you might enjoy. YouTube tracks what you watch and recommends related videos. Each of these online services uses machine learning to try to turn you into a long-term customer or user.

Other organizations are using machine learning for automatic translation. YouTube might use it to transcribe video and generate captions. Some sites use a very similar machine learning technology to translate captions into different languages. Through natural language processing (NLP), powered by machine learning, some services translate captions into a synthesized voice that sounds similar to a human being.

With machine learning, computers tap the power of artificial intelligence to process massive data sets and extract valuable information from that data. They can find connections in the data that humans could never detect on their own and may never think to look for. Sometimes we can understand how these intelligent computers made the connection and other times we cannot.

One of the most interesting aspects of machine learning is that it doesn't replicate human learning; it's a completely different way to find connections, make decisions and gain greater understanding. So if you're planning to use machine learning in your organization, you have to start thinking about how machines learn, so you can start to collect data that will help the machine learn to perform the task you need it to perform.

Machine learning didn't start to really gather steam until companies had large datasets, and that's not a coincidence; data is the fuel that drives machine learning. That's why some of the first companies that benefited from machine learning were the ones that had access to massive datasets. Data plays a crucial role in what the machine learns, how well it learns, and how fast it learns. Usually, the more data you have, and the better that data is, the sooner the machine will start delivering useful insights.

So before you start your machine learning project you should think about your data. Is it high quality? Do you have enough for the computer to learn something new? Is the dataset broad enough to accurately represent whatever you're asking the machine to examine? The broader the view, the more likely it is to find something interesting. You don't want your program looking through a keyhole. If you plan to use this technology, think about some strategies for collecting diverse, high-quality datasets.

Chapter 2: The process of neural networks

We can talk about neural network architecture now that you know more about deep learning and its applications. Neural networks are very important for machines. A properly programmed neural network will help the machine think like a person and process information in that way. These networks are made out of layers. These layers can process many kinds of information. Each layer is made out of neurons that all work together to solve problems. Since neural networks help machines think like humans, it makes sense that machines with neural networks are capable of learning. Pattern recognition and data classification are some of the things that these machines are used for.

When neurons change and adjust, the network can learn, similar to human beings.

A person who does not dabble with AI, somebody that you may talk to on the street, could be shocked to learn that they have encountered a lot of artificial intelligence and other kinds of machine learning. Millions of dollars are spent by some of the most popular companies in order to research that will improve their business. Some of these companies are Apple, Google, Facebook, Amazon, and IBM.

Our day to day lives might be impacted by this research already, even though you might not know it. With internet searches, for example, you will be shown options on websites and searches that match the keywords you typed in. Machine learning is important for this as it is the main thing that allows your browser to filter through the millions of possible recommendations.

The same principle is used in Netflix recommendations or spam filters that help filter through your emails. In the medical industry, this is used for the classification of medication and has an important role in the Human Genome Project where it goes through the countless combinations of patterns in DNA that can tell you something about your family history, risk factors, or health prospects.

These systems are applicable in most industries as they are highly adaptable and sophisticated. This is made possible through algorithms that guide the computer through many learning processes. With the correct algorithms, you can teach a system to detect abnormal behaviors that can happen within a pattern. This helps the system learn how to predict possible outcomes that may occur in a wide variety of situations.

An artificial neural network is something that contains algorithms of different kinds, data receptors and a plethora of other elements. Ever since they were introduced during the 1950s, artificial neural networks have been a remedy when it comes to the future of science. They are patterned similarly to the human brain.

They allow the machine to learn during the training phase of programming. This knowledge is then used as a foundation for solutions that would be applied to problems in the future.

Historical Background

Neural networks have been a thing since before computers. The problem was that people were not proficient enough for utilizing them. This is why the recent advances made in the field of neural networks are so important. Any developments in computer technologies help the research of neural networks. A craze started and people started being enthusiastic over the field. However, most attempts were fruitless, as no advancements that could help to improve the efficiency and accuracy of our machines. The enthusiasm started to decrease. However, some of the researchers remained steadfast and continued their studies. They worked hard in order to develop what we have now, a technology model that is accepted by most people in the industry.

The first artificial neural network was made by Warren McColloch and Walter Pitts in the year 1943. This was called the McCulloch-Pitts neurons. The network was not used to perform or automate complex tasks as the duo did not have the technology needed for the further development of the network.

What Are They and How Do They Work?

Terms like artificial intelligence, machine learning, and deep learning are all terms that refer to processes that are happening in and to the neural network. People might be skeptical when it comes to the way machines learn. However, we assure you that it really means that they are trained like human minds are.

A computational distributed model is made up of simple parallel processors with a plethora of tiny connections is a good way to think about these networks. The human brain is made from many, many neurons that are interconnected via synapses which allow them to make analysis and computations in our cerebral cortex. Learning is achieved with the change in the connections in our brains allow us to acquire new skills and learn new skills so that we can solve difficult problems.

A good way to think of these networks is to think of many simple parallel processors integrated with hundreds (or thousands) of tiny connections that make up a computational distributed model. In the human brain, there are millions of neurons all interconnected by synapses that allow them to make computations and analysis in the cerebral cortex. As these connections are made, learning is achieved allowing the person to acquire new skills so they can accomplish complex problems.

Hundreds of homogenous processing units that are interconnected through links are elements of a neural network. The unique configurations of connections and simplicity are what make this design truly beautiful. Data goes into the network through an input layer and goes to the output layer. In the meantime, the data is processed through the many layers in between until the problem is computed and a final solution is carried out.

Only a few units that transfer information were the gist of the structure of the simple neural networks in their earlier days. Today, however, a network could be made up of millions of different units that are intertwined and work together in order to emulate the process of learning. More modern networks are able to solve very difficult and complex problems in many ways.

Why use Neural Networks?

Large volumes of data are dedicated to making improvements to the industry by the industry itself. There are many variables in these datasets that can make it difficult for humans to find patterns in that appear in the datasets themselves. Via neural networks, we can recognize these patterns more easily. Without them, computers could find it to be a difficult task to identify trends in the dataset. By taking the time to train a neural network, an engineer can feed the network huge datasets in order to turn it into an expert in a selected area. With this trained network, the engineer can predict the output for any possible input. This also allows the engineer to be able to answer some questions about the future. Neural networks have many advantages and here are some of them:

• A neural network can adapt to new tasks and learn how to do new things because of it using supervised machine learning

• The network can be used to report back any information that was fed to it during the learning stage

• Machines with neural network architecture work far faster and provide more accurate results. This is because of the ability to compute data in parallel.

• Neural networks can be fixed fairly easily. While performance will be affected if the network is damaged, the network will still remember some of the properties.

The McCulloch-Pitts Neuron - What is It?

There are a lot of similarities between the human brain and artificial neural networks. This makes sense due to the fact that these networks were made to emulate how the human brain This much is easy to understand. The following are some of the similarities between them:

• Millions of artificial neurons make them up and each one of them can compute problems and solve them

• Each neuron has many different connections

• They are both non-linear and parallel

- They can learn through the change in the connection between units
- They adapt to new knowledge when they find an error instead of penalizing themselves
- Based on the data that they never came across before, they can produce outputs

These all describe how the neural network, as a whole, works. While the two are very similar on the surface, we should look into how the smallest of the units work. The McCulloch-Pitts neuron is the smallest part of the network. In the brain, the basic unit of processing is a neuron. In the artificial neural network, this unit is the main part of processing any type of information and calculations of any kind. It is made from the following three elements:

- The weight and synaptic efficacy of connections, as well as the connections themselves
- An agent that summarizes and processes input signals and outputs linear combinations
- A system that limits the neuron's output

The 1940s was the first time that the MCP neuron was introduced. This neuron got its name from the logician Walter Pitts and the neuroscientist Warren S. McCulloch. They tried to understand what happens inside of the human brain when we try to produce and understand complex patterns and replicate them through the connections between the many basic cells.

The design of old systems was very simple. The input was quantified from zero to one and the output was limited to the same domain. Every input was either inhibitory or excitatory. This simplicity made the design limited the learning capabilities of the machine.

While sometimes simplicity can be great, it also has its downfalls. It costs the computational ability to comprehend complex topics.

The MCP neuron was supposed to sum up all of the inputs. The neuron takes all of the positives and negatives that appear and compiles them, adding plus one if an input is positive and taking one away if the input is negative.

Neural Networks versus Conventional Computers

Neural networks and computers do not apply the same kind of solution to every problem. The latter usually use algorithms in order to find solutions. Conventional computers also have another method of solving a problem. If you taught it the steps that it should follow it should do good by them in order to find a solution. What this tells us is that humans and computers can solve similar problems. Where computers shine is solving problems that people can't.

As we have said numerous times, the human brain and neural networks work in a similar manner: through a network of interconnected neurons. These networks usually work in parallel for the best efficiency. An engineer can teach a network to complete a task by giving it an example of how it should approach the solution. This means that selecting the data you feed to the system is very important. If you are not careful when selecting the data you might make it harder for the system to learn the process. The networks are unpredictable as, due to the data they are fed, it might learn to solve problems that the engineer didn't foresee.

Computers apply some cognitive approaches when solving problems, as well. If the engineer gives the computer proper instructions the computer can act on them and solve problems. Using a high-level programming language, it takes only a few steps for the engineer to provide the instructions to the computer. The computer, later, takes these instructions and translates it into a language that the computer can understand. This process allows the engineer to predict how the computer will go about solving certain problems. If the computer reports a problem while processing, the engineer can conclude that there should be an error in the software or hardware.

Conventional computers work in tandem with neural networks. Arithmetic calculations are a kind of task that is best solved by conventional algorithmic computers. On the other hand, other, more complex tasks, can be solved by neural networks most efficiently. Most tasks are best solved by combining the two approaches so that the machine can work at peak efficiency,

Types of Neural Networks

Fully connected neural network

A network layer is the most basic type of neural network architecture. It is composed out of three layers of neurons which are interconnected. The input layer is the first layer. It is connected to a hidden layer of neurons which then proceed to the output layer. The input layer is where the engineer gives data to the system. The nodes that connect the hidden layer and the input layer dictate how the input layer views the data it is given. What kind of data outputted depends on the weights and connections between the secret layer and output layer.

This kind of architecture is simple, but still interesting because the hidden layers can represent data in many ways. The weights mentioned before are nodes that connect layers. They also determine when these layers need to be activated. An engineer can modify these weights and change the way the layers interact. He can do this to ensure the way the hidden layer shows data is conducted the correct way.

It is fairly easy to tell a multilayer and single-layer architecture apart. When it comes to single-layer architecture, neurons are connected at the nodes. This means that the processing power of the network is maximized due to all of the layer being interconnected. When it comes to multilayer architecture there are more layers to the system. Here neurons are not interconnected, but the layers are.

Perceptrons

The term perception was coined in 1960 by Frank Rosenblatt. This happened during a time where neural network architecture developed greatly. Perceptions represent a kind of McCulloch and Pitts model which is assigned a pre-processing and fixed weight. This makes the system easier to use when it comes to recognizing the patterns, resembling the function in human beings. This network can be used in other processes too.

Feed-forward Networks

There are several names for this kind of network. Bottom-up or top-down are both alternative names for feed-forward networks. This means that signals and data will flow in only one direction, from the input point to the output point. This network does not have a feedback loop. This means that output gotten in one instance will not affect output that comes in another layer. This is one of the simplest networks to make as input is directly associated with output. This network is often used in recognizing patterns.

Convolutional neural networks

Fully connected neural networks are what convolutional neural networks bears the most similarity to. Many layers made from many neurons are what makes up this system. Each neuron is assigned with a weight. This is due to the training data that was used during the teaching phase. When input is given to a neuron they will make a dot product, which is followed by a non-linearity. You might wonder what the difference between a fully connected neural network and a convolutional network is. A CNN views each input in the original dataset to be an image which an engineer can encode properties of the system into. This reduces the number of instances in the original dataset and it makes it easier for the network to use the forward function. These types of neural networks are used by most deep learning programs.

Feedback networks

Feedback networks are specific due to the movement of the signals. They flow in both directions and induce a loop into the network. These networks are extremely difficult to make, but are very powerful. The network will function in a state of absolute equilibrium until you create a change. This state of constant change will continue until the system equalizes again. If an engineer feeds a new dataset to the system, it will try to find a new point of equilibrium. This is the reason why feedback networks are recurrent and interactive. Below we will discuss recurrent neural networks.

Recurrent neural networks

Recurrent neural networks are special because the information always loops. The network will consider the input and asses what it has learned, once it decides. RNN usually has short-term memory. In combination with Long Short-term memory, it gains long-term memory. We will further discuss this bellow.

It is difficult to explain RNN without using an example. Let's say that the network you are using is a regular feed-forward neural network. Let's say that you input the word "brain". The system will separate the word into characters and go over them one by one, always forgetting the previous characters. This means that this model cannot be used to predict which character is next unless it has already been gone over. Due to its internal memory, an

RNN remembers previous characters and predicts the next ones. While producing outputs, it copies them and puts them back into the network itself. This means that RNNs will produce, on top of the present information, five immediate past information. Due to all of this, the following inputs are all a part of an RNN:

- The Present Data
- The Recent Data

As always, the dataset selection is very important. The dataset used to teach the model will affect how the system uses sequences while predicting upcoming characters in a text. This places RNN in front of most algorithms when it comes to the functions they can perform. Unlike a feed-forward network, RNN applies weight to both the previous and current input data and shifts the weights that have already been assigned, while a feed-forward network assigns weights to neurons in each layer in order to produce and output.

Generative adversarial network

A GAN, also known as a generative adversarial network, is made up of two networks that have been pitted against each other. Due to this, we call it an adversarial network. GAN can be used by most engineers in a system, because it can learn to mimic any distribution or dataset. GAN can be used to build something that is unique to you in many domains. It can simultaneously process pictures, prose, speech, etc. You are bound to be impressed by the output of these networks.

A generator and a discriminator are parts of this network. The discriminator evaluates instances made by the generator, while the generator creates the data instances themselves. The discriminator's job is to identify if a new instance is from a premade training dataset or not.

Training the Neural network

Training your neural network is one of the most important parts of making a neural network. There are a few methods to do this, however, only one method has the most positive results. Error backpropagation, also known as the error propagation algorithm, symmetrically adjusts the weights on connections and neurons. This means that if the system makes a mistake it will learn from it and come closer to the correct solution every time.

This kind of training has two stages: stage 1, also known as the forward propagation, and stage 2, also known as back propagation.

In stage 1, a calculation of all of the activated neurons in all of the layers is performed. During this stage, there is no change to synaptic connection weights. What this means is that the default values will be used in the first iteration of the system. During phase 2, however, we are given an actual answer from the network and we can compare the output to the expected output in order to determine the error rate.

The error rate is then taken into account and it is returned to one of the synaptic connections. Modifying the weights then decreases the difference between the expected value and the value we got. This process happens on and on until the error margin is decreased to the point where it can't be decreased anymore.

• Forward Propagation: in forward propagation, the first input is the initial data that is then transferred to the hidden layers where it is processed until an output is produced. The activation functions, the depth of the data, and the width of the data all depend on the basic architecture of the network. Depth tells us how many hidden layers exist within the system. The width tells us the number of neurons in each layer and the activation functions instruct the system on exactly what to do.

• Backward Propagation: It allows for the weight of the connections to be adjusted via a supervised learning algorithm. This is done in order to reduce the difference between the solution we got and the expected solution.

Neural networks are a very interesting field of study and keeps getting more and more intricate, now using machine learning. It has a huge amount of potential to aid the creation of future developments in computer science.

• They are adept at solving problems whose solutions require a certain degree of error

• They can use experience from solving previous problems and use it to solve problems it encounters for the first time.

• Their implementation is a piece of cake as the definitions for duplication, neurons, and creating connections are easy to understand

• It completes operations fairly quickly as every neuron operates on only the value it received as input

• Stable outputs directly relate to the input values

• Before producing a result, they can take all of the inputs into accounts

Neural networks still have a few drawbacks, even with all of those advantages. Some of them are:

• It has a certain similarity to black boxes. You can determine what happened, but there is no way to determine why a certain result was produced

• The memory cannot be described or localized in the network itself

• They can only be used by computers with compatible hardware as they have unique computer needs

• Producing proper calculations can be very time consuming, however, as the training techniques are extensive and can take a while to execute.

• The only method of solving problems is algorithms

and you have to give them the correct one for the problem
- The accuracy of the output values can vary
- A large number of examples is needed for a good learning process that can produce solutions to be made
Neural networks are completely capable of independent decision making based on the number of inputs and variables. Because of this, they can create an unlimited number of recurring iterations to solve problems without human interference. When we see these networks in action, you'll find a numeric vector that represents the various types of input data. These vectors could be anything from pixels, audio and/or video signals, or just plain words. These vectors can be adjusted via a series of functions producing an output result.

At first glance, you might think that there is not that much to say about neural networks. However, when you look into it a bit more, you start to see the intricacies behind it. The same system can be used to handle the most basic of problems and the most complex alike. The only thing that changes is the number of weights that are placed on each value.

We have already pointed out that these algorithms are an integral part of machine learning. They are used to sift through all sorts of data, pull out any information that could be useful to reach the targeted goal and bring you to the closest possible solution to a problem. All of this is done without having to write a specific code for the computer to actually solve the problem because of something called a 'neural network'.

But what exactly is a neural network? Let's go back and take another look at the human brain so we can get a better understanding of this new technology.

The brain holds billions of tiny little neurons that are

poised to receive data and process it. These neurons are all interconnected through a complex web with each neuron holding a certain amount of information. These neurons send signals to each other as they process the data they receive.

In a computer, a neural network is created artificially. The architecture has been around for decades but the technology has advanced enough just recently for it to be implemented into any usable and functional form.

In an artificial neural network (ANN) these neurons are mimicked by thousands (sometimes millions) of tiny little processing units, all linked together. Each one of these artificial neurons has a purpose, which is determined by the configuration or the topology of the network.

There are several layers of these neurons and each layer has its own specific purpose. There is the input layer, where all the data flows into the network, the output layer where the solution is produced, and there could be numerous hidden layers where much of the processing work is done.

Training and Selection of a Predictive Model

As we will see in the next sections, various machine learning algorithms have been developed with the aim of solving different problems. An important element that can be drawn from David Wolpert's well-known No Free Lunch Theorems is that there is no "free" learning. For example, each classification algorithm has its inherent flaws, and no classification model can claim absolute superiority if we have no information on the task at hand. In practice, it is therefore essential to compare at least a certain group of different algorithms, so as to train them and then select the model that offers the best performance. But before we can compare different models, we need to decide which metrics to use to measure performance. A commonly used metric is the accuracy of the classification, which is defined as the proportion between the instances correctly classified.

A legitimate question arises: how can we understand which model performs better on the final test dataset and on the real data if we do not use this test dataset for choosing the model, but we keep it for the final evaluation of the model itself? In order to solve the problem inherent in this question, various cross-validation techniques can be used, in which the training dataset is further subdivided into subsets of validation training, in order to estimate the performance of generalization of the model. Finally, we cannot even expect that the standard parameters of the various learning algorithms provided by software libraries are optimal for our specific problem. Therefore, we will frequently use hyper-parameter optimization techniques, which will help us optimize the performance of the model. Intuitively, we can consider these hyper-parameters as parameters that are not learned from the data but represent the "knobs" of the model, on which we can intervene to improve their performance, as we will see with greater clarity in the next sections when we will put them to work on examples effectively.

Evaluation of Models and Forecasting Of Data Instances Never Seen Before

It is important to note that the parameters of the procedures we have just discussed (reduction of the scale and size of the features) can only be obtained from the training dataset and that these same parameters are then reapplied to transform the test dataset and also each new sample some data. Otherwise, the performance measured on the test data could be overly optimistic.

Chapter 3:Learn coding with python

When Guido van Rossum developed the first Python language compiler in the late 1980s, little did he know that the language will be more famous than popular languages in machine learning and Artificial Intelligence. The fact is—in the last couple of years; Python language has emerged as a solution for most machine learning problems.

Python language is beginner-friendly, yet very powerful. It is no wonder that Python language is finding its applications in some of the most popular systems such as Google, Pinterest, Mozilla, Survey Monkey, Slideshare, YouTube, and Reddit as a core developer language. Also, Python's syntax is extremely simple to understand and follow if you're a beginner or advanced programmer.

If you're an advanced developer of C, C++, Java or Perl, you'll find programming in Python to be extremely simple. If you're an experienced developer, you can accomplish great things with Python. Besides developing games, data analysis, and machine learning, Python language can also be used to code general AI systems and development of GUIs.

This chapter explores how you can engineer ML systems in Python language. Let's get started.

Getting started with Python

Obviously, to kick start developing machine learning systems in Python, you need to install it on your computer and set the programming environment. If you're a novice Python programmer, learning basics of Python installation and setting up the environment will go a long way in promoting your bottom line.

The installation process

The process of downloading and installing the Python language interpreter is pretty simple. If you're using the latest Linux distribution—whether it's Ubuntu, Fedora or Mint—then you'll find the most recent version of Python already installed. All you have to do is to update your system. If you're using a Debian-based Linux distribution, follow these steps to update your system:

· Launch the Terminal app and type the following command at the command prompt:

su apt-get update

· Type your root password and press the Enter key
· Wait for the update process to be completed.

If you're using a Redhat-based Linux distribution such as Fedora, follow these steps to update your system:

· Launch the Terminal app and type the following command at the command prompt:

su apt-get update

· Type your root password and press the Enter key
· Wait for the update process to be completed.

On the other hand, if you're using other OS's apart from Linux, you have to download and install Python yourself. Also, if you're using an older version of Linux that has no Python, then you have to install it manually.

Follow the steps outlined below to install Python on Linux distributions:

· Launch the Terminal app (Ensure that you're connected to the internet)
· Type "su" at the command prompt and press the enter key
· Type your root password and hit the enter key
· If you're using Debian-based Linux distribution such as Ubuntu, then type: "apt-get install python" at the command prompt and press the enter key
· On the other hand, if you're using the Red Hat/ RHEL / CentOS Linux distributions such as Fedora, then type: "yum install python" at the command prompt and

hit the Enter key.

- Wait for the installation to complete.
- Update the system by typing: "su apt-get update" if you're using Debian-based Linux distributions or "su yum update" if you're a Redhat/ RHEL / CentOS Linux distribution user.

What about Windows OS?

Before you download and install Python, decide on the version of Python language that you would want to install. As a rule of thumb, always go for the latest version. As of writing this book, the latest version was 3.6.2. Here are steps that can help you install Python on Windows OS:

- Go to www.python.org and download the current version of Python. Select the appropriate version depending on the nature of your OS (32 bit, or 64 bit).
- Open the Python file that you've just downloaded
- Click on the "Accept the default settings" from the on-screen instructions and wait for the installation process to complete.

If you're a Mac OS X or Sierra user, then you'll find Python 2.7 already portedto the OS. Therefore, you don't have to install or configure anything if you want to begin using Python. However, if you wish to install the latest version of Python, you need to use the Homebrew. Here are steps that can help install Python on your Mac OS:

- Open your Terminal or any of your favorite OSX terminal emulator
- Type the following command at the command prompt:"/user/bin/ruby-e"$(curl-fsSL https://raw.githubusercontent.com/Homebrew/install/master/install)".
- Now proceed to install Python language interpreter by typing the following command at the command prompt: "brew install python."

- Wait for the installation process to complete.

Now that you've installed Python, what next?

It's now time to begin developing your ML systems. But not that fast! You should decide on what text editor you'll use. You can opt to select your best editors to help you code and execute your program. Some of the most popular Text Editors are Emacs, Geany, Komodo Edit and Sublime Text.

But since we all know the pitfalls of the Text Editors—such as running the code manually from the Python Shell—I won't advise you to use them. Instead, use the Python IDLE (Integrated Development Environment). I have been using it ever since without problems. However, you can choose an IDE that suits you.

Python IDLE has the following features:
- Syntax highlighting
- Auto-completion of code statements
- Smart indentation
- Integrated debugger with the stepping, persistent breakpoints, and call stack visibility features.

Launching Python

To get started, you have to understand how to launch the Python app. You can launch Python from the Terminal or use the desktop environment for starting the IDLE app. Simply launch the Terminal and type: "idle" at the command prompt. Now that you've launched the Python, it's now time to begin coding.

Let's now create our first program in Python. Follow these steps to write your first Python program:
- Open the Python IDLE.
- Write the Python language statements (instructions) in the IDLE window.
- Run the program

That's it! Simple. Isn't it?

Now, here's a quick way to see the programming process in action...Proceed and copy/paste the following code into your Python IDLE window.

```
print ("Hello World! This is my first Machine Learning program")
```

Run the program. What do you see as the output?

Well, the phrase "Hello World! This is my first Machine Learning program" appears.

Congratulations! You've just written your first Python code. I know you're now excited to begin coding ML systems. Don't worry so much about the meaning of statements. If you are a machine learning novice, mastering some Python programming concepts will help you understand how to design ML applications.

Next up, let's dive in together and get to the basics of Python programming.

An Overview of Python

Now that you have executed your first Python program, what else do you need to know? Well, it's now time to understand the vital components of any Python code including its structure. All Python programs have the following structure:

```
import sys
def main ():
main ()
{
Program statements
}
```

As you can see from this program structure, all Python codes should always start with the keyword "import." Now, what are we importing? Python language is object-oriented. Therefore, it has components of all the object-oriented programming languages. One such property is inheritance or in simple terms; code reuse. The ability to inherit features of codes in Python allows programmers to reuse pieces of codes that had been written elsewhere.

Technically speaking, the import statement tells the Python interpreter to declare classes that have already been used in other Python packages without referring to their full package names. For instance, the statement: "import sys" informs the interpreter to include all the system libraries such as print whenever the Python program is starting.

What does the statement "def main ( ):" mean?

Whenever a Python program is loaded and executed, the computer's memory—the Random Access Memory—contains the objects with function definitions. The function definitions provide the programmers with the capabilities of instructing the control unit to place the function object into the appropriate section of the computer's memory. In other words, it's like instructing the control unit to check the main memory and initialize the program that needs to be executed.

The function objects in the memory can be specified using names. That's where the statement "def main ( ):" comes in. It simply tells the control unit to start executing the Python code statements that are placed immediately after the statement "def main ( ):"

For example, the Python code below creates a function object and assigns it the name "main":

```
def main ():
  if len (sys.argv) == 10:
    name = sys.argv [2]
  else:
    name = "Introduction to Machine Learning."
    print ("Hello"), name
```

In the above code, the Python interpreter will run all the

function statements in the Python file by placing the set of functions objects in the memory and linking each of them with the namespace. This will happen when the program is initialized with the import statement.

But more fundamentally, "What are the different elements of Python code?" Well, all Python programs have the following components:

· Documenting the program. Any statement in the program (except the first) that starts with "#" is treated as a command line or comment line and will be ignored during execution. This will allow you to comment on sections of the code for proper documentation.

· Keywords. The keywords are instructions that the interpreter recognizes and understands. For instance, the word "print" in the earlier program is a keyword. In Python, there are two main types of keywords: the functions and the control keywords. Functions are simple verbs such as print that tell the interpreter what to do while the control keywords control the flow of execution.

· Modules. Python program is shipped with a large list of modules that increase its functionality. The modules will help you to organize your code in a manner that's easy to debug and control the code.

· Program statements. The program statements are sentences or instructions that tell the control unit to perform a given operation. Unlike most programming languages, the Python statements don't need a semicolon at the end.

· Whitespace. The white spaces are a collective name that given to tabs, the spaces, and newlines/carriage returns. The Python language is strict on where the white space should be placed in the code.

· Escape sequences. The Escape sequences are special characters that are used for output. For instance:

the sequence "\n" in the program tells Python to output on a new line.

Python variables

There's so much that goes on in the main memory of the computer whenever you run a program. Understanding the concept of variables and data types will help you to write efficient programs.

A program is simply a sequence of instructions (statements) that directs your computer to perform a particular task. For instance, the previous program printed the phrase "Hello World! This is my first program" on the screen when it was executed. But before you could see the output on the screen some data had to be kept in computer's memory.

The use of data applies to all programming languages— Python included—therefore, understanding the mechanisms of data management in the computer's memory is the first step towards developing robust, efficient and powerful applications.

A variable can be conceived as a temporary storage location in the computer's main memory and specifically the Random Access Memory. This temporary storage location is what will hold the data that you would like to use in the program. In other words, the variable location of memory that holds data whenever your program is executing. So, whenever you define a variable, you'll actually be reserving a temporary storage location in the computer's memory.

All the variables that you define must have names and an equivalent data type— a sort of classification of the variable that specifies the type of value the variable should hold. The data types help to specify what sort of mathematical, relational or even logical operations that you can apply to the variable without causing an error.

Ideally, when you assign variables to data types, you can begin to store numbers, characters, and even constants in the computer's main memory.

Since Python language is an oriented programming language, it is not "statically typed." This means that the interpreter regards every variable as an object. Therefore, you have to declare the variables before using them in your program. So, how can you declare variables in Python?

Names or identifiers usually declare Python variables. Just like any other programming languages that you have so far learned, the conventions for naming the variables must strictly be adhered to. Below are some naming conventions that you should follow when declaring variables:

· All variable names should always begin with a letter (A to Z and a to z) or an underscore. For instance, "age" is a valid variable name while "-age" isn't a valid variable name.

· Any variable name you declare cannot start with a number. For instance, 9age is not a valid variable name.

· Special symbols shouldn't be used when declaring variable names. For instance, @name isn't allowed as a variable name.

· The maximum number of characters to use for your variable name shouldn't exceed 255.

To reserve a temporary memory location in the name of a variable, you don't have to use the explicit declaration like other programming languages. If you've had experience in other programming languages such as Pascal or C, I am sure you know that declaring a variable explicitly before assigning any value is a must.

In Python, the declaration of variables usually occurs automatically the moment you assign a value to it. For instance, the statement;

age=10

Automatically reserves a temporary storage location in memory space called "age" and assigns 10 to it.

It is also possible to assign a single value to several variables simultaneously. For instance, the statement below reserves temporary memory spaces for 2 variables namely: age and count and assigns the value 30:

age, count=30

Python language has different categories of data types that are used to define the storage methods and mathematical operations. Below are examples data types in Python language:

- Numbers
- String
- List
- Tuple
- Dictionary

*a)	Numbers*

The Number data types stores numeric values. The number objects will automatically be initialized whenever you assign a specific value to the variable. For instance, the code illustrated below creates 2 variable objects (age and count) and assigns them the values 10 and 30 respectively:

age = 10

count= 30

If you want to delete reference to the Number object, you'll use the word "del" followed by the variable name that you wish to delete. Consider the code below that deletes two variables: age and count that have already been declared and used."

del age, count

Python language supports four different categories of number types. These are:
· int. when used in a declaration it refers to signed integers. These include those whole numbers that range from 8 bits to 32 bits.
· long. These are long integers. They can be represented either in octal and hexadecimal numbering notation.
· float. These are floating real point values. They may range from 8 bits to 64 bits long.
· complex. These are complex numbers.

b)   *Strings*

Strings are stored as consecutive sets of characters in the computer's memory locations. Python language allows you to use either pair of single or double quotes when defining the strings. Other subsets of string variable types can be specified using the slice operator ([ ] and the [:]) with the indexes that range from 0 at the beginning of the string. The plus (+) operator performs string concatenation (joining of two or more strings) while the asterisk (*) operator performs string repetition.

File Handling in Python

A file is simply a named location on disk that has stored related information. Files are used to store data on a permanent basis on a non-volatile storage device such as a hard disk. You are aware that the main memory—and specifically the RAM—can't be used to store data on a permanent basis. Therefore, files must always be stored on a permanent storage device.

When a file is created on a secondary storage device, the following file information is automatically generated by the respective OS:
· Name of the file
· Its location

- File size
- File attributes such as read/write read only and archive

You can use this mode if you are dealing with non-text data such as images.

The File Object Attributes

Once you've opened a file, the file object is created automatically with the following information that is related to the file.

The Python code below illustrates an example of how you can work with file object attributes:

```
myfile = open("Readme.txt", "wb")
print "The name of the file is: ", myfile.name
print "Is the file closed or not? : ", myfile.closed
print "The opening mode of the file is: ", myfile.mode
print "The Softspace flag of the file is: ," myfile.softspace
```

The above code will produce the following output:

The name of the file is: Readme.txt

Is the file closed or not? : False

The opening mode of the file is: wb

The Softspace flag of the file is:

The close() Method

The close() method of a file object is used to flush any unwritten information and close the file object. When the file has been closed, no more writing can take place. You should note that Python automatically closes the file when the reference object of the file is reassigned to another file. That is why it is a good programming practice to use the close() method to close a file.

Below is the syntax for closing a file:

```
fileObject.close()
```

Below is an example code of how you can close a file in Python:

```
myfile = open("Readme.txt", "wb")
```

print "The name of the file is: ", Readme.name
myfile.close()
Reading and Writing Files
The file object gives a set of access methods that make the process of reading and writing to files much easier. In particular, the two methods that you'll need are read() and write() methods.
The write method
Here's the syntax for the write() method:
fileObject.write(string)
Below is an example of a Python code that uses the write() method:

```
myfile = open("Readme.txt", "wb")
myfile.write( "I have learned several aspects of Python Programming in this book.\n And the book is great for Advanced Programmers! \n")
myfile.close()
```

The above method creates a Readme.txt file and writes the given content in that file. When you finally open the file, here will be its contents:
I have learned several aspects of Python Programming in this book. And the book is great for Advanced Programmers!
The read method
The read () method is used to read a string from a file that you have opened. It is crucial to note that Python strings can also have binary data, apart from the text data. Below is its syntax:
fileObject.read([count])
In the above example, the passed parameter is the number of bytes that are supposed to be read from the opened file. The read method begins reading from the start of the file, and if the count is missing, then it will

attempt to read as much information as possible until the end of the file.

Here is an example:

```
myfile = open("Readme.txt", "r+")
mystr = myfile.read(10);
print "Read string is: ", mystr
# Check current position
position = myfile.tell();
print "Current file position : ", position
# Reposition the pointer at the start of the string once again
position = myfile.seek(0, 0);
mystr = myfile.read(10);
print "Again read Mystring is: ", mystr
# Close the opened file
myfile.close()
```

Looking at the above code, you'll realize that you have to create a loop for you to read the entire string. One easy way to read the text file and parse each line the statement readlines on with the file object. The Python's readlines reads every data in the in the text file. Here's an example:

```
myfile = open("Readme.txt", "r")
lines = myfile.readlines()
f.close()a
```

Now the above code reads the entire file

What about reading the file line by line?

You can use the while statement to help you read file line by line. Below is an example:

```
myfile = open("Readme.txt")
line = myfile.readline()
while line:
    print line
    line = myfile.readline()
myfile.close()
```

Up to this point, we've only described Python language in terms of structure, some elementary data structures, and file handling. I believe this is necessary to get you started with engineering machine learning system. However, what we've covered isn't exhaustive. Truth be told—there's so much to learn in Python. For you to master machine learning, you've to dig deeper into Python programming.

Have you been using the classification as a type of machine learning? Probably yes, even if you did not know about it. Example: The email system has the ability to automatically detect spam. This means that the system will analyze all incoming messages and mark them as spam or non-spam.

Often, you, as an end user, have the option to manually tag messages as spam, to improve the ability to detect spam. This is a form of machine learning where the system takes the examples of two types of messages: spam and so-called ham (the typical term for "non-spam email") and using these cases automatically classify incoming mails fetched.

What is a classification? Using the examples from the same domain of the problem belonging to the different classes of the model train or the "generate rules" which can be applied to (previously unknown) examples. Dataset Iris is a classic collection of data from the 1930s; This is one of the first examples of modern statistical classifications. These measurements allow us to identify the different types of flower.

Today, the species are identified through DNA, but in the 30s the role of DNA in genetics had not yet been recorded. Four characteristics were selected for each plant sepal length (length of cup slip) sepal width (width of cup slip) petal length, and petal width. There are three classes that identify the plant: Iris setosa, Iris versicolor, and Iris virginica.

Formulation of the problem

This dataset has four characteristics. In addition, each plant species was recorded, as well as the value of class characteristics. The problem we want to solve is: Given these examples, can we anticipate a new type of flower in the field based on measurements?

This is the problem of classification or supervised learning, where based on the selected data, we can "generate rules" that can later be applied to other cases. Examples for readers who do not study botany are: filtering unwanted email, intrusion detection in computer systems and networks, detection of fraud with credit cards, etc.

Data Visualization will present a kind of triangle, circle type, and virginica type of mark x.

The model has already discussed a simple model that achieves 94% accuracy on the entire data set. The data we use to define what would be the threshold was then used to estimate the model.

What I really want to do is to assess the ability of generalization model. In other words, we should measure the performance of the algorithm in cases where classified information, which is not trained, is used.

Transmitting device stringent evaluation and use the "delayed" (Casually, Held-out) data is one way to do this.

However, the accuracy of the test data is lower! While this may surprise an inexperienced person who is engaged in machine learning, it's expected to be lower by veterans. Generally, the accuracy of testing is lower than the accuracy of training. Using the previous examples you should be able to plot a graph of this data. The graph will show the boundary decisions.

Consider what would happen if the decision to limit some of the cases near the border were not there during the training? It is easy to conclude that the boundaries move slightly to the right or left.

NOTES: In this case, the difference between the accuracy of the measured data for training and testing is not great. When using a complex model, it is possible to get 100% accuracy in training and very low accuracy testing! In other words, the accuracy of the training set is a too optimistic assessment of how good your algorithm is. Experiments always measured and reported the accuracy of testing and accuracy on the set of examples that are not being used for the training!

A possible problem with the hold-out validation is that we are only using half of the data used for training. However, if you use too much data for training, assessment error testing is done on a very small number of examples. Ideally, we would use all the data for the training and all the data for testing, but it was impossible.

A good approximation of the impossible ideals is a method called cross-validation. The simplest form of cross-validation is Leave-one-out cross-validation.

When using cross-checking, each example was tested on a model trained without taking into account that data. Therefore, cross-validation is a reliable estimate of the possibilities of generalization model. The main problem with the previous method of validation is a need for training of a large number (the number grows to the size of the set).

Instead, let's look at the so-called v-fold validation. If,

for example, using 5-fold cross-validation, the data is divided into five parts, of which in each iteration 4 parts are used for training and one for testing.

The number of parts in the initial set of components depends on the size of the event, the time required for the training model, and so on. When generating fold data, it is very important to be balanced.

You may also start to notice that there are many different companies, from startups to more established firms, that are working with machine learning because they love what it is able to do to help their business grow. There are so many options when it comes to working with machine learning, but some of the ones that you may use the most often are going to include:

• Statistical research: machine learning is a big part of IT now. You will find that machine learning will help you to go through a lot of complexity when looking through large data patterns. Some of the options that will use statistical research include search engines, credit cards, and filtering spam messages.

• Big data analysis: many companies need to be able to get through a lot of data in a short amount of time. They use this data to recognize how their customers spend money and even to make decisions and predictions about the future. This used to take a long time to have someone sit through and look at the data, but now machine learning can do the process faster and much more efficiently. Options like election campaigns, medical fields, and retail stores have used machine learning for this purpose.

• Finances: some finance companies have also used machine learning. Stock trading online has seen a rise in the use of machine learning to help make efficient and safe decisions and so much more.

As we have mentioned above, these are just three of the ways that you are able to apply the principles of machine learning in order to get the results that you want to aid in your business or even to help you create a brand new program that works the way that you want. As technology begins to progress, even more, you will find that new applications and ideas for how this should work are going to grow as well.

Data modeling is an important aspect of Data Science. It is one of the most rewarding processes that receive the most attention among learners of Data Science.

However, things aren't the same as they might look because there is so much to it rather than applying a function to a given class of package.

The biggest part of Data Science is assessing a model to make sure that it is strong and reliable. In addition, Data Science modeling is highly associated with building information feature set. It involves different processes which make sure that the data at hand is harnessed in the best way.

Robust Data Model

Robust data models are important in creating the production. First, they must have better performance depending on different metrics. Usually, a single metric can mislead the way a model performs because there are many aspects in the classification problems.

Sensitivity analysis describes another important aspect of Data Science modeling. This is something that is important for testing a model to make sure it is strong. Sensitivity refers to a condition which the output of a model is meant to change considerably if the input changes slightly. This is very undesirable because it must be checked since the robust model is stable. Lastly, interpretability is an essential aspect even though it is not always possible. This is usually related to how easy one can interpret the results of a model. But most modern models resemble black boxes. This makes it hard for one to interpret them. Besides that, it is better to go for an interpretable model because you might need to defend the output from others.

How Featurization Is Achieved

For a model to work best, it must require information that has a rich set of features. The latter is developed in different ways. Whichever the case, cleaning the data is a must. This calls for fixing issues with the data points, filling missing values where it is possible and in some situations removing noisy elements.

Before the variables are used in a model, you must perform normalization on them. This is achieved using a linear transformation on making sure that the variable values rotate around a given range. Usually, normalization is enough for one to turn variables into features once they are cleaned.

Binning is another process which facilitates featurization. It involves building nominal variables which can further be broken down into different binary features applied in a data model.

Lastly, some reduction methods are important in building a feature set. This involves building a linear combination of features that display the same information in fewer dimensions.

Important Considerations

Besides the basic attributes of Data Science modeling, there are other important things that a Data Scientist must know to create something valuable. Things such as in-depth testing using specialized sampling, sensitivity analysis, and different aspects of the model performance to improve a given performance aspect belong to Data Science modeling.

To help you understand just how deep the field of deep learning goes and just how much it has changed everyone's lives already, I will dedicate this section to showing you specific examples of deep learning and how it is used in its myriad of applications.

Keep in mind, this is not meant to advertise any kind of product or service, but to show you that deep learning is far more common than many people think and that it is not a field pertaining to the higher levels of each industry, but one that belongs to all of us to some extent.

So, without further ado, let's dive in:

Image Curation on Yelp

Although Yelp may not be as popular as it used to be, it still has a very important role to play in how people experience the new places in their living areas (or the different locations they visit as tourists, for example).

At first, Yelp may seem like anything but a tech company - but they are using actual machine learning to make sure their users come back to the site because it provides them with actual, helpful information.

More specifically, Yelp has developed a machine learning system capable of classifying, categorizing, and labeling images submitted by users - but more importantly, this system helps Yelp do this in a genuinely efficient way. This is extremely important for the company, given the huge amounts of image data they receive every day.

Pinterest Content

Who knew searching for wedding ideas on Pinterest is

fueled by machine learning?

Pinterest's main purpose is that of curating existing content - so it makes all the sense in the world that they have invested in machine learning to make this process faster and more accurate for their users.

The system developed by Pinterest is capable of moderating spam and helping users find content that is more relevant to their own interests, their styles, and their searches.

Facebook's Chatbots

By this point, it is more than likely that you have stumbled upon at least one chatbot in Facebook Messenger.

These apparently simplistic chatbots are, in fact, a form of primordial artificial intelligence. Sure, Skynet is not typing from the other end of the communication box, but even so, chatbots are a fascinating sub-field of artificial intelligence - one that is developing quite steadily.

Facebook Messenger allows any developer to create and submit their own chatbots. This is incredibly helpful for a variety of companies that emphasize their customer service and retention, because these chatbots can be used for this precise purpose. Sometimes, Messenger chatbots are so well-built that you may not even realize that you are talking to a, "robot."

Aside from chatbots, Facebook invests a lot in developing AI tools capable of reading images to visually impaired people, tools capable of filtering out spam and bad content, and so on.

In some ways, a company that might not seem to have a lot to do with technological innovation is pushing the boundaries of one of the most exciting fields of the tech world: artificial intelligence.

Google's Dreamy Machines

Google is one of the companies constantly investing in artificial intelligence (often, with amazing results). Not only have they developed translation systems based on machine learning, but pretty much every area of their activity is somewhat related to artificial intelligence too. Don't be fooled - Google has its hands in much more than search engines. In recent years, they have invested a lot in a very wide range of industries, including medical devices, anti-aging tech, and, of course, neural networks.

The DeepMind network is, by far, one of the most impressive neural network research projects ran by Google. This network has been dubbed as the "machine that dreams" when images recreated by it were released to the public, opening everyone's eyes to how artificial intelligence, "perceives" the world.

Baidu Voice Search

Since China is the leading country in artificial intelligence research, it only makes sense that their leading search company, Baidu, is heavily invested in the realm of artificial intelligence too.

One of the most notable examples here is their voice search system which is already capable of mimicking human speech in a way that makes it undistinguishable form, well, **actual** human speech.

IBM's Watson

We couldn't have missed Watson from this list, mostly because this is one of the first impressively successful artificial intelligence endeavors in history.

Most people know IBM's Watson from its participation in **Jeopardy!**, but the supercomputer built by the super tech giant IBM can do **much** more than just compete in televised shows.

In fact, Watson has proved to be very useful to

hospitals, helping them propose better treatment in some cancer cases. Given the paramount importance of this type of activity in medicine, it can be said that Watson helps to save actual lives - which is a truly great example of how AI can serve mankind.

Salesforce's Smart CRM

Salesforce is one of the leading tech companies, specifically in the field of sales and marketing, where the tool helps businesses maximize their sales potential and close more deals with their customers.

Salesforce is based on a machine learning tool that can predict leads and assigns scores for each of them. For sales people and marketing pros, this is a true gold mine because it makes the entire sale process smoother, more fluent, and, overall, more efficient.

Where Do You Come From, Where Do You Go, Deep Learning?

Clearly, deep learning advances are quite fascinating. Many take them for granted simply because the speed at which they have developed in recent years means that every year brings a new tool to the market - a tool to use in medicine, healthcare, business, commerce, and more.

The future of deep learning cannot be predicted with certainty - if we had an ultra-powerful AI, it might be able to make an accurate prediction of what will happen next. Even so, **human brains** figure that the following will happen over the next few years:

Better Learning

The more they learn, the more powerful machines become. We have a long way to go before we see the first full AI that is capable of mimicking thought processes and emotions - but the more AI is learning, the faster it will continue to grow.

As I was saying earlier in this book, it is a snowballing effect - so the more the "machine learning ball" is rolling, the larger it will become, and the more strength it will have.

Better Cyber Attack Protection

While humans might be able to beat codes created by humans, it might be a little more difficult for hackers to break in when an AI is protecting the realms of data held by a company. Soon enough, artificial intelligence will be capable of better monitoring, prevention, and responses when it comes to database breaches, DDoS attacks, and other cyberthreats.

Better Generative Models

Generative models aim to mimic human beings as much as they can, in very specific areas. The Baidu example in the previous section is a very good indicator here. Over the next few years, we will start to see a lot more of these very convincing generative models, to the point where we will not be able to make a clear distinction between humans and machines (at least in some respects).

Better Training for Machines

Machine learning training is fairly new, given the rapid ascension of this industry in the past couple of decades. The more we train our machines, however, the better we will become at it - and this means that the machines themselves will be able to make better, more accurate decisions.

Chapter 4: The programmatic way

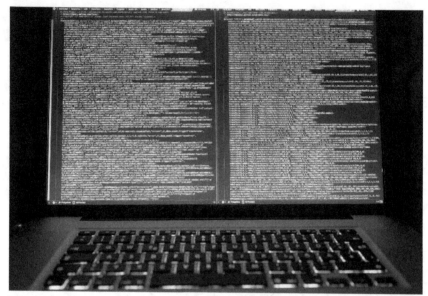

There are many models of Machine Learning. These theoretical describe the heuristics used to accomplish the ideal, allowing the machine to learn on their own. Below is a list and description of some of the most popular.

Decision Tree

Just about everyone has used the decision tree technique. Either formally or informally, we decide on a single course of action from many possibilities based on previous experience. The possibilities look like branches and we take one of them and reject the others.

The decision tree model gets its name from the shape created when its decision processes are drawn out graphically. A decision tree offers a great deal of flexibility in terms of what input values it can receive. As well, a tree's outputs can take the form of a category, binary, or numerical. Another strength of decision trees is how the degree of influence of different input variables can be determined by the level of decision node in which they are considered.

A weakness of decision trees is the fact that every decision boundary is a forced binary split. There is no nuance. Each decision is either yes or no, one or zero. As well, the decision criteria can consider only a single variable at a time. There cannot be a combination of more than one input variable.

Decision trees cannot be updated incrementally. That is to say, once a tree has been trained on a training set, it must be thrown out and a new one created to tackle new training data.

Ensemble Methods address many tree limitations. In essence, the ensemble method uses more than one tree to increase output accuracy. There are two main ensemble methods — bagging and boosting.

The bagging ensemble method (known as Bootstrap Aggregation) is mean to reduce decision tree variance. The training data is broken up randomly into subsets and each subset is used to train a decision tree. The results from all trees are averaged, providing a more robust predictive accuracy than any single tree on its own.

The boosting ensemble method resembles a multi-stage rocket. The main booster of a rocket supplies the vehicle with a large amount of inertia. When its fuel is spent, it detaches and the second stage combines its acceleration to the inertia already imparted to the rocket and so on. For decision trees, the first tree operates on the training data and produces its outputs. The next tree uses the earlier tree's output as its input. When the input is in error the weighting it is given, makes it more likely the next tree will identify and at least partially mitigate this error. The end result of the run is a strong learner emerging from a series of weaker learners.

Linear Regression

The premise of linear regression methods rests on the assumption that the output (numeric value) may be expressed as a combination of the input variable set (also numeric). A simple example might look like this:

x = a1y1, a2y2, a3y3...

Where x is the output, a1...an are the weights accorded to each input, and y1...yn are the inputs.

The strength of a linear regression model lies in the fact it can produce well in terms of scores and performance. It is also capable of incremental learning.

A weakness of the linear regression model is the fact that it assumes linear input features, which might not be the case. Inputs must be tested mathematically for linearity.

K-Means Clustering Algorithm

K-Means clustering algorithms can be used to group results that talk about similar concepts. So, the algorithm will group all results that discuss jaguar as an animal into one cluster, discussions of Jaguar as a car into another cluster, and discussions of Jaguar as an operating system into a third. And so on.

Neural Network

We have covered neural networks in detail above. The strengths of neural networks are their ability to learn non-linear relationships between inputs and outputs.

Bayesian Network

Bayesian networks produce probabilistic relationships between outputs and inputs. This type of network requires all data to be binary. The strengths of the Bayesian network include high scalability and support for incremental learning. We discussed Bayesian models in more detail earlier in the book. In particular, this Machine Learning method is particularly good at classification tasks such as detecting if an email is or is not spam.

Python programming language does not allow special characters such as @, $, /, and % within identifiers. Python is a case sensitive programming language.

Therefore, identifiers such as 'Python' and 'python' are two different identifiers in Python programming language.

Below are the naming conventions for identifiers in Python.

- Class name in Python always begins with an uppercase letter and all other Python identifiers starts with a lowercase letter.

- A Python identifier is private when such identifier begins with a single leading underscore.

- A Python identifier is strongly private when such identifier begins with two leading underscores.

- A Python identifier is a language-defined special name when such identifier ends with two trailing underscores.

Python Reserve Words

Reserve words in any programming language are special commands that compiler or interpreters understands, and these reserve words cannot be used as a constant or variable, or any other identifier names in that programming language.
Python has the following reserve words, and all such keywords contain lowercase letters only.

Python Keywords

Representing a Statement as Multi-Line

Statements in the Python language ends with a new line. If the statement is required to be continued into the next line, then the line continuation character (\) is used in Python language. This line continuation character (\) denotes that the statement line should continue as shown in the below screenshot. In the below example, we have three variables result1, result2 and result3 and the final output is copied to the variable named result. Instead of writing the equation statement in a single line (result=result1+result2+result3), here, we have used line continuation character (\) so that, it could be written in three lines but represents a single statement in Python language.

Also, a Python statement which is defined within braces (), {} and [] does not require the line continuation character (\) when written as a multi-line statement. This kind of Python statements are still interpreted as a single statement without the use of the line continuation character (\).

Quotation in Python

The Python language permits the use of single ('), double (") and triple (''' or """) codes to represent a string literal, making sure that the same type of quote begins and ends that string. In the below example, single, double and triple codes are used to represent a string in a word, sentence or paragraph. When we print this variable, they print the string irrespective of single, double and triple codes used for representing string literal in Python language.

Comments in Python

Any comment in the Python language is represented by a hash sign (#) provided it is not used inside a string literal between codes (single, double or triple). All characters after the hash sign (#) and up to the end of the physical line are the part of comment and Python interpreter ignores this statement while interpreting the whole program. In the below example, the interpreter will just print the string present inside the print command and will ignore the parts mentioned after a sign before and after as comments.

Using Blank Lines

A blank line in the Python language is either a line with white spaces or a line with comments (i.e. statement starting with a hash sign (#)). The Python interpreter while interpreting a blank line, ignores it and no machine readable code will be generated. A multiline statement in Python is terminated after entering an empty physical line.

Waiting for the User

Using the Python programming language, we can set up the prompt which can accept a user's input. The following line of the program will display a prompt, which says "Press any key to exit", and waits for the user input or action.

Multiple Statements on a Single Line

The Python language allows to write multiple statements on a single line if they are separated by a semicolon (;) as demonstrated in the example below.

Command Line Arguments

On UNIX OS, which has Python interpreter installed, we can take help and see all the lists of the functions. These are the basic ones. The below screenshot demonstrates the help command on the UNIX system and all the functions or short codes used.

Machine Learning and Robotics

First, we need to define a robot. They are machines, often programmable by a computer, that are able to carry out a series of complex actions without intervention. A robot can have its controls systems embedded or be controlled by an external device. In popular literature and film, many robots are designed to look like people, but in fact, they are usually designed to perform a task and that requirement determines how they appear.

Robots have been with us for almost as long as computers. George Devol invented the first digitally operated and programmable one in 1954, called Unimate. In 1961, General Motors bought it to use for lifting hot metal die castings. And like computers, robots have changed our society. Their strength, agility, and ability to continue to perfectly execute the same repetitive tasks have proved an enormous benefit. And while they did cause some serious disruption to the manufacturing industries, putting many people out of work, their ascension in our societies has provided far more employment opportunities than they have taken.

Robots in current use can be broken down into several categories:

Industrial Robots/Service Robots

These robots are probably familiar. You have likely seen them on the television or streaming video of automated factories. They usually consist of an "arm" with one or more joints, which ends with a gripper or manipulating device. They first took hold in automobile factories. They are fixed in one location and are unable to move about. Industrial robots will be found in manufacturing and industrial locations. Service robots are basically the same in design as industrial robots but are found outside of manufacturing concerns.

Educational Robots

These are robots used as teacher aids or for educational purposes on their own. As early as the 1980s, robots were introduced in classrooms with the turtles, which were used in classrooms where students could train them using the Lego programming language. There are also robot kits available for purchase like the Lego Mindstorm.

Modular Robots

Modular robots are consisted of several independent units that work together. They can be identical or have one or more variation in design. Modular robots are able to attach together to form shapes that allow them to perform tasks. The programming of modular robotic systems is of course, more complex than a single robot, but ongoing research in many universities and corporate settings is proving that this design approach is superior to single large robots for many types of applications. When combined with Swarm Intelligence (see below), modular robots are proving quite adept at creative problem-solving.

Collaborative Robots

Collaborative robots are designed to work with human beings. They are mostly industrial robots that include safety features to ensure they do not harm anyone as they go about their assigned tasks. An excellent example of this kind of collaborative robot is Baxter. Introduced in 2012, Baxter is an industrial robot designed to be programmed to accomplish simple tasks but is able to sense when it comes into contact with a human being and stops moving.

Of course, all the examples above do not require any artificial intelligence. When robots are coupled with machine learning, researchers use the term "Robotic Learning". This field has a contemporary impact in at least four important areas:

Vision

Machine Learning has allowed robots to visually sense their environment and to make sense of what they are seeing. New items can be understood and classified without the need to program into the robot ahead of time what it is looking at.

Grasping

Coupled with vision, Machine Learning allows robots to manipulate items in their environment that they have never seen before. In the past, in an industrial factory, each time a robot was expected to interact with a different-shaped object, it would have to be programmed to know how to manipulate this new object before it could be put to work. With Machine Learning, the robot comes equipped with the ability to navigate new item shapes and sizes automatically.

Motion Control

With the aid of Machine Learning, robots are able to move about their environments and avoid obstacles in order to continue their assigned tasks.

Data

Robots are now able to understand patterns in data, both physical and logistical, and act accordingly on those patterns.

Example of Industrial Robots and Machine Learning

One example of the benefit of applying Machine Learning to robots is of an industrial robot which receives boxes of frozen food along a conveyor. Because it is frozen, these boxes often have frost, sometimes quite a lot of frost. This actually changes the shape of the box randomly. Thus, a traditionally-trained robot with very little tolerance for these shape changes would fail to grasp the boxes correctly. With Machine Learning algorithms, the robot is now able to adapt to different shapes, random as they are and in real time, and successfully grasp the boxes.

Another industrial example includes a factory with over 90,000 different parts. It would not be possible to teach a robot how to manipulate these many items. With Machine Learning, the robot is able to be fed images of new parts it will be dealing with and it can determine its own method to manipulate them.

In 2019, there will be an estimated 2.6 million robots in service on the planet. That's up a million from 2015. As more and more robots are combined with Machine Learning algorithms, this number is sure to explode.

There are a lot of reasons you may want to Python. Or, you may just be looking for a place to start with the wide, wide world of programming. Regardless of your specific purpose and goal, I can guarantee you that the Python programming language will provide you with all of the tools that you need to do exactly what it is that you want to do.

If you're browsing the introductory pages of this book on a preview or something of the like, on the fence as to whether or not you want to learn Python, well, I can tell you that you probably should.

See how much easier it is? And this is just with rudimentary programming concepts. When you get into heavier programming concepts like variables, functions, and other things of that nature, Python actually goes out of the way to make them really simple and functional to handle. We'll get more into this in the other chapters, of course.

On top of this, Python, as I've already said, is a language which has endless opportunity for usage and growth.

There are very few explicitly **bad** situations for Python. This makes it a great language to learn initially for the simple fact that you'll be able to get a ton of mileage out of it. There will be very few times where, as a beginning programmer, you'll come up with a concept you'd like to carry out that you **won't** be able to conquer perfectly well with Python.

So enough of all that, how do we get started with Python? Well, you're going to need a few things first. Of course, you're going to need a computer, preferably with an active internet connection, but there are going to be more things that you need.

Let's start our programming adventure right here. I'm going to teach you everything that you need to get going with Python, so just follow along.

The first thing that you're going to need to grab is Python itself. You can get it by going to the Python website at http://python.org. You'll be able to download and install it for your respective operating system. Note that this isn't entirely relevant if you're working on Linux or macOS. Most versions of these operating systems will generally have a version of Python on it. You may, though, need to downgrade. If so, you're going to need to search for instructions which are relevant to your specific operating system because the instructions can vary depending upon which operating system you're using.

If you don't know whether Python is pre-installed or not, you can figure it out by going to either the Terminal (in macOS or Linux systems) or elevated Powershell (in Windows) and running the command "python". If your instance of Terminal or Powershell says something along the lines of "Command not recognized", then congratulations, you need to install Python. If it recognizes the command and says "Python 3.x.x" in the program initiation text, you need to downgrade.

Anyhow, on the Python site, you need to be certain that you're getting Python version 2.7.12, and **not** Python version 3. This is for one simple reason: Python 2 and 3 are a bit different in the way that they handle certain core functions. Not glaringly so, but one of the reasons that someone learns to program is so that they can speak directly to the computer. Learning Python 2 will give you many more opportunities to do this. This is for the simple reason that it's been **around** longer. There's much more code written for Python 2 than Python 3. You'll be able to work with a lot more code if you learn to work with Python 3 first. Now, granted, Python 3 is of course bleeding edge. But when you're learning to program, bleeding edge is not always best. It's preferable here that you learn how to read and write and deal with more code than you would otherwise. Basically, you're trying to cover as much ground with as little as possible when you're starting out, and Python 2 accommodates you for that goal perfectly. The few things you'll have to learn or relearn for Python 3 once you're more experienced with Python or programming in general will be non-factors compared to trying to understand deprecated code samples from Python 2 which aren't relevant to the code that you're trying to write.

With that out of the way, once you have Python 2.7.13 (or the latest version of Python 2 available) installed, you're going to need to get a text editor. It doesn't matter exactly what text editor you use, there are several good different candidates. The one I specifically recommend to use is called Atom, and you can get it at http://atom.io. There are a few reasons that I recommend this one. Firstly, it's free. What's better than high quality free software? Secondly, it's super simple to use and jam packed with features right out of the box, yet without being a sort of bloated and ugly software. Thirdly, it's incredibly extensible: there's nigh endless support for it through various different extensions and things of the sort online. There's so much that you can do with Atom. The endless possibilities of it and Python complement each other perfectly. And last but not least, you can get it for every major operating system.

Once you have Atom and Python installed, let's get right down to business on your first program. I'd recommend firstly that you create a new folder on your computer in an easily accessible place like the desktop or high up on your C drive. Name it something along the lines of Python. I don't recommend adding spaces in the name because it will slow down the process of navigating to it by just a little bit. Anyway, after you do that, you're going to open Atom. Once it's open, you're going to right click on the sidebar and click "Add Project Folder". Then you navigate to the project folder on your computer and select it. Then, you double click the folder in the sidebar in order to make it the active folder, and you right click on the sidebar and select "New File". Then after that, you're going to type hello.py.

In the file, you're going to type the following:
print "hello world!\n"

Then go ahead and save. Open up your Terminal or Powershell in order to run this. Navigate to the file you just made. If you don't know how to navigate in the command line, it's a worthwhile skill for any programmer in the making. If you don't know how to get around in the command line, then you need to. You can find a lot of useful and simple guides on Google that can teach you the basics in no time. I'm sorry to keep delegating things to Google searches, but it's really just that these topics go far beyond the scope of this book and, in the interest of staying focused and on topic, I think it's pertinent that I stay relevant to the topics at hand.

Anyway, you're going to navigate to the file and run it with the following command:

python hello.py

If everything goes according to plan, then you should get an output just like this:

hello world!

If that's the case, then congratulations! You just wrote your very first Python program. You've taken the first crucial steps to being a fully able programmer. It's all uphill from here.

Chapter 5: Organize data using effective pre-processing techniques

Data processing is the act of changing the nature of data into a form that is more useful and desirable. In other words, it is making data more meaningful and informative. By applying machine learning algorithms, statistical knowledge, and mathematical modeling, one can automate this whole process. The output of this whole process can be in any form like tables, graphs, charts, images, and much more, based on the activity done and the requirements of the machine.

This might appear simple, but for big organizations and

companies like Facebook, Twitter, UNESCO, and health sector organizations, this whole process has to be carried out in a structured way. The diagram below shows some of the steps that are followed:

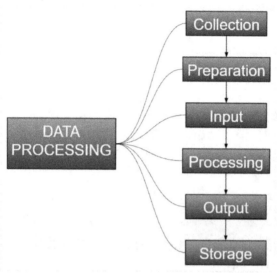

Let's look in detail at each step:

Collection The most important step when getting started with Machine Learning is to ensure that the data available is of great quality. You can collect data from genuine sources such as Kaggle, data.gov.in, and UCI dataset repository. For example, when students are getting ready to take a competitive exam, they always find the best resources to use to ensure they attain good results. Similarly, accurate and high-quality data will simplify the learning process of the model. This means that during the time of testing, the model would output the best results.

A great amount of time, capital, and resources are involved in data collection. This means that organizations and researchers have to select the correct type of data which they want to implement or research.

For instance, to work on the Facial Expression Recognition requires a lot of images that have different human expressions. A good data will make sure that the results of the model are correct and genuine.

Preparation

The data collected can be in raw form. Raw data cannot be directly fed into a machine. Instead, something has to be done on the data first. The preparation stage involves gathering data from a wide array of sources, analyzing the datasets, and then building a new data set for additional processing and exploration. Preparation can be done manually or automatically and the data should be prepared in numerical form to improve the rate of learning of the model.

Input

Sometimes, data already prepared can be in the form which the machine cannot read, in this case, it has to be converted into readable form. For conversion to take place, it is important for specific algorithm to be present. To execute this task, intensive computation and accuracy is required. For example, you can collect data through sources like MNIST, audio files, twitter comments, and video clips.

Processing

In this stage, ML techniques and algorithms are required to execute instructions generated over a large volume of data with accuracy and better computation.

Output

In this phase, results get procured by the machine in a sensible way such that the user can decide to reference it. Output can appear in the form of videos, graphs, and reports.

Storage

This is the final stage where the generated output, data

model, and any other important information are saved for future use.

Data Processing in Python

Let's learn something in python libraries before looking at how you can use Python to process and analyze data. The first thing is to be familiar with some important libraries. You need to know how you can import them into the environment. There are different ways to do this in Python.

You can type:

From math import *

In the first way, you define an alias m to library math. Then you can use different functions from the math library by making a reference using an alias m. factorial ().

In the second method, you import the whole namespace in math. You can choose to directly apply factorial () without inferring to math.

Note:

Google recommends the first method of importing libraries because it will help you tell the origin of the functions.

The list below shows libraries that you'll need to know where the functions originate from.

NumPy: This stands for Numerical Python. The most advanced feature of NumPy is an n-dimensional array. This library has a standard linear algebra function, advanced random number capability, and tools for integration with other low-level programming languages.

SciPy: It is the shorthand for Scientific Python. SciPy is designed on NumPy. It is among the most important library for different high-level science and engineering modules such as Linear Algebra, Sparse matrices, and Fourier transform.

scikit-learn: This is designed for machine learning. It was created on matplotlib, NumPy, and SciPy. This specific library has a lot of efficient tools for machine learning and statistical modeling. That includes regression, classification, clustering, and dimensionality community.

StatsModels: This library is designed for statistical modeling. Statsmodels refers to a Python module which permits users to explore data, approximate statistical models, and implement statistical tests.

Other libraries

- Requests used to access the web.
- Blaze used to support the functionality of NumPy and Pandas.
- Bokeh used to create dashboards, interactive plots, and data applications on the current web browsers.
- Seaborn is used in statistical data visualization.
- Regular expressions that are useful for discovering patterns in a text data
- NetWorx and Igraph applied to graph data manipulations.

Now that you are familiar with Python fundamentals and crucial libraries, let's now jump into problem-solving through Python.

An exploratory analysis in Python with Pandas

If you didn't know, Pandas is an important data analysis library in Python. This library has been key at improving the application of Python in the data science community. Our example uses Pandas to read a data set from an analytics Vidhya competition, run exploratory analysis, and create a first categorization algorithm to solve this problem.

Before you can load the data, it is important to know the two major data structures in Pandas. That is Series and DataFrames.

Series and DataFrames

You can think of series as a 1-dimensional labeled array. These labels help you to understand individual elements of this series via labels.

A data frame resembles an Excel workbook, and contains column names which refer to columns as well as rows that can be accessed by row numbers. The most important difference is that column names and row numbers are referred to as column and row index.

Series and data frames create a major data model for Pandas in Python. At first, the datasets have to be read from data frames and different operations can easily be subjected to these columns.

Import libraries and data set

This chapter will use the following python libraries:

- **NumPy**
- **Matplotlib**
- **Pandas**

Once you have imported the library, you can move on and read the dataset using a function read_csv(). Below is how the code will look till this point.

```python
import pandas as pd
import numpy as np
import matplotlib as plt
%matplotlib inline
#Reading the dataset in a dataframe using Pandas
df = pd.read_csv("/home/kunal/Downloads/Loan_Prediction/train.csv")
```

Notice that the dataset is stored in
Once you read the dataset, you can decide to check a few
top rows by using the **function head().**
Next, you can check at the summary of numerical fields
by using the **describe () function.**

Distribution analysis

Since you are familiar with basic features of data, this is
the time to look at the distribution of different variables.
Let's begin with numeric variables-ApplicantIncome and
LoanAmount.

First, type the commands below to plot the histogram of
ApplicantIncome.

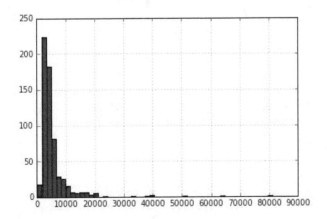

Notice that there are a few extreme values. This is why
50 bins are needed to represent the distribution clearly.

The next thing to focus on is the box plot. The box plot for fare is plotted by:

```python
df.boxplot(column='ApplicantIncome')
```

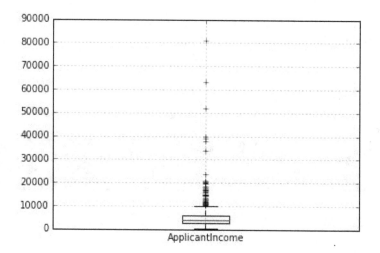

This is just a tip of an iceberg when it comes data processing in Python.
Let's look at:

Techniques for Preprocessing Data in Python

Here are the best techniques for Data Preprocessing in Python.

1. Rescaling Data

When you work with data that has different scales, you

need to rescale the properties to have the same scale. The properties are rescaled between the range 0 to 1 and refer to it as normalization. To achieve this, the MinMaxScaler class from scikit-learn is used.

```
>>> import pandas, scipy, numpy
>>> from sklearn.preprocessing import MinMaxScaler
>>> df=pandas.read_csv( 'http://archive.ics.uci.edu/ml/machine-learning-databases/wine-quality/winequality-red.csv ',sep=';')
>>> array=df.values
>>> #Separating data into input and output components
>>> x=array[:,0:8]
>>> y=array[:,8]
>>> scaler=MinMaxScaler(feature_range=(0,1))
>>> rescaledX=scaler.fit_transform(x)
>>> numpy.set_printoptions(precision=3) #Setting precision for the output
>>> rescaledX[0:5,:]
```

For example:

```
>>> rescaledX[0:5,:]
array([[0.248, 0.397, 0.   , 0.068, 0.107, 0.141, 0.099, 0.568],
       [0.283, 0.521, 0.   , 0.116, 0.144, 0.338, 0.216, 0.494],
       [0.283, 0.438, 0.04 , 0.096, 0.134, 0.197, 0.17 , 0.509],
       [0.584, 0.11 , 0.56 , 0.068, 0.105, 0.225, 0.191, 0.582],
       [0.248, 0.397, 0.   , 0.068, 0.107, 0.141, 0.099, 0.568]])
```

After rescaling, you get the values between 0 and 1. By rescaling data, it confirms the use of neural networks, optimization algorithms as well as those which have distance measures such as the k-nearest neighbors.

2. Normalizing Data

In the following task, you rescale every observation to a specific length of 1. For this case, you use the Normalizer class. Here is an example:

```
>>> from sklearn.preprocessing import Normalizer
>>> scaler=Normalizer().fit(x)
>>> normalizedX=scaler.transform(x)
>>> normalizedX[0:5,:]
```

```
>>> normalizedX[0:5,:]
array([[2.024e-01, 1.914e-02, 0.000e+00, 5.196e-02, 2.079e-03, 3.008e-01,
        9.299e-01, 2.729e-02],
       [1.083e-01, 1.222e-02, 0.000e+00, 3.611e-02, 1.361e-03, 3.472e-01,
        9.306e-01, 1.385e-02],
       [1.377e-01, 1.342e-02, 7.061e-04, 4.060e-02, 1.624e-03, 2.648e-01,
        9.533e-01, 1.760e-02],
       [1.767e-01, 4.416e-03, 8.833e-03, 2.997e-02, 1.183e-03, 2.681e-01,
        9.464e-01, 1.574e-02],
       [2.024e-01, 1.914e-02, 0.000e+00, 5.196e-02, 2.079e-03, 3.008e-01,
        9.299e-01, 2.729e-02]])
```

3. Binarizing Data

If you use the binary threshold, it is possible to change the data and make the value above it to be 1 while those that are equal to or fall below it, 0. For this task, you use the Binarized class.

```
>>> from sklearn.preprocessing import Binarizer
>>> binarizer=Binarizer(threshold=0.0).fit(x)
>>> binaryX=binarizer.transform(x)
>>> binaryX[0:5,:]
```

```
>>> binaryX[0:5,:]
array([[1., 1., 0., 1., 1., 1., 1., 1.],
       [1., 1., 0., 1., 1., 1., 1., 1.],
       [1., 1., 1., 1., 1., 1., 1., 1.],
       [1., 1., 1., 1., 1., 1., 1., 1.],
       [1., 1., 0., 1., 1., 1., 1., 1.]])
```

As you can see, the python code will label 0 over all values equal to or less than 0, and label 1 over the rest.

4. Mean Removal

This is where you remove mean from each property to center it on zero.

5. One Hot Encoding

When you deal with a few and scattered numerical values, you might need to store them before you can carry out the One Hot Encoding. For the k-distinct values, you can change the feature into a k-dimensional vector that has a single value of 1 and 0 for the remaining values.

```
>>> from sklearn.preprocessing import OneHotEncoder
>>> encoder=OneHotEncoder()
>>> encoder.fit([[0,1,6,2],
[1,5,3,5],
[2,4,2,7],
[1,0,4,2]
])
```

6. Label Encoding

Sometimes labels can be words or numbers. If you want to label the training data, you need to use words to increase its readability. Label encoding changes word labels into numbers to allow algorithms operate on them. Here's an example:

```
>>> from sklearn.preprocessing import LabelEncoder
>>> label_encoder=LabelEncoder()
>>> input_classes=['Havells','Philips','Syska','Eveready','Lloyd']
>>> label_encoder.fit(input_classes)
```

Machine learning Projects

You can read volumes of theory, but that can never help you build confidence in the subject when compared to hands-on practice. Most people believe that they become masters when they read textbooks and articles. But, when they try to apply the theory, they notice that it is harder than it looks.

When you work on projects, you improve your skills and have the chance to explore interesting topics. You can also add these projects to your portfolio, which will make it easier for you to land a job.

Data Analysis

The data analysis project is one that most people begin with since it helps to hone some statistical skills. By working on this project, you can build your practical intuition around machine learning. The goal of this exercise is to help you use different models and apply those models to a variety of datasets. There are three reasons why you should begin with this project.

• You will learn to identify which model will fit your problem. For example, some datasets may have missing information. When you work on this project, you will know which model you should use for such datasets. You can always dig through texts and articles to learn which model is better, but it is better to see it in action.

• You will develop the art of creating prototypes of models. It is often difficult to identify if a model will work best for the problem without trying it.

• You must keep the process flow or workflow of the machine in mind when you build a model. You will master this technique when you work on this project. For example, you can practice:

How to import data

Which tools should you use to clean data

How to split the data into training sets

Pre-processing of data

What transformations must you make to the data

Since you use different models, you can focus on the development of the skills mentioned above. For instructions, you can look at the Python (sklearn) and R (caret) documentation pages. You must also practice classification, clustering and regression algorithms.

Social Media

Social media is synonymous with big data because of the volumes of content that users generate. You can mine this data and keep tabs on trends, public sentiments and opinions. Facebook, YouTube, WhatsApp, Instagram and many other platforms have data that you can use to achieve your objective.

Social media data is important for branding, marketing and for a business since every generation spends more time on social media when compared to its preceding generation. Twitter is one of the platforms you should start with when you begin to practice machine learning. You have interesting data sets and metadata that can open an endless path for analysis.

Fantasy Leagues or Sports Betting

If you have read the book Moneyball, you know how the Oakland A's changed the face of baseball through their analytical scouting. Based on the analysis, the team built a highly competitive squad and bought the players for almost a third of the price when compared to the Yankees players. If you have not read the book yet, you must grab a copy and read it now.

There are large volumes of data in the sports world that you can play with. You can use data for games, teams, players and scores to analyze patterns. These data are available online. For instance, you can try the following projects and see where they lead you.

You can bet on specific box scores in different games based on the data available on the Internet right before a game begins. You can analyze the data and identify where you should place your bets to increase your chances of winning.

You can scout for talent in schools and colleges using the statistics for different players. This analysis can help college scouts identify the players they want on their team.

You can become a manager for a fantasy team and use your analysis to win games and leagues.

The sports domain is especially useful since it helps a beginner practice exploratory analysis and data visualization. These skills will help you identify what types of data you should include in your analysis.

Stock Market

An aspiring data scientist will always base his projects on the stock market since that is like Disneyland for them. The stock market is an interesting area to work on since you have different types of data available. You can find data on fundamentals, prices, stocks, economic scenarios, macroeconomic and microeconomic indicators, volatilities and many more.

The data available is granular which makes it easier for people to obtain historical data, also called time series data, for every company. Using this data, you can build creative trading strategies. Since financial markets have small cycles, you can validate any prediction you make immediately.

You can analyze the data and assess the movement of prices for different stocks for a period of 6 months. You should use the quarterly reports provided by the company to make this prediction.

You can use a time series models and recurrent neural network models to forecast the correlation between the stock prices. You can also assess the volatility of the prices.

It is simple to build a financial trading model to improve your skills in machine learning. However, it is difficult to profit from these models here. Experts recommend that you do not use real money to trade until you have perfected the model.

Writing Machine Learning Algorithms

It is important for a beginner to learn how to write machine learning algorithms from scratch for two reasons:

There is no better way to understand the mechanics of the algorithms since you must think about the process flow of the algorithm thereby helping you master algorithms.

You can translate statistical and mathematical instructions into working code, which allows you to apply algorithms in your academic research.

It is best to start off with simpler algorithms since you must make hundreds of decisions. Once you are comfortable with simple algorithms, you can extend the functionality of those algorithms to complex algorithms like regression and clustering.

Your packages may be slow and may not be as fancy as the algorithms in existing packages. It took the developers years to build these packages.

Chapter 6:Getting grip to a deeper textual and social media data

Machine learning technological approach is radically different from the way companies traditionally exploit data. Instead of starting with business logic and applying the data, machine learning techniques allow data to create logic. One of the key benefits of this approach is the removal of commercial assumptions and prejudices that may lead managers to customize a strategy that may not be the best.

THE IMPACT OF MACHINE LEARNING ON APPLICATIONS

We boldly stated that with machine learning, you start with the data and let the data take you to logic. How does a company achieve the goal? As with all the development and deployment of complex applications, you need a planning process to understand the business issue to be solved and to collect the appropriate data sources.

The formulas used are pretty basic, most of them are not different from what you learned in high school. The difference is that computers can do them much faster than we can with our human minds. Even if we are the best at figuring out these types of math problems, humans can never calculate them as quickly as a computer can. Our minds aren't built that way. While it may take us a minute or so to calculate a few numbers in our head, computers have the capability of figuring out millions of equations in a fraction of the time.

But that does not mean that computers are an improved version of the human mind. There are things that the human mind can do equally fast that computers have yet to figure out. Actions like pattern recognition, unstructured problem solving and functioning in 3-dimensional space. Yes, more advanced computers can perform these types of tasks and solve problems, but they have to be given structure and parameters in areas where rules must be followed. Human minds are flexible enough to adapt their thinking to varying circumstances in a vast array of areas. Yes, computers can operate cars and come to quick conclusions, but they have difficulty multitasking and maneuvering in areas without bumping into things or encountering an error.

However, with each passing year, the latest computers are capable of doing more and more things that they could never do in the past. It seems to be just a matter of time before they will one day be capable of doing everything that humans can do but much faster and far more efficiently.

Chapter 7: Optimize your machine learning systems and algorithms

You will find that with machine learning, it is important to recognize that there will be a relationship that will form between this process and the probability theory. Machine learning can be a broad field, and this means that it can intersect with some other fields. The fields that it interacts with will depend on the specific project you will work with. Probability and statistics often merge with machine learning so understanding how these three can work together can be important for your project.

There are a few different ways that statistics and the probability theory will be really important to the whole learning process that goes on with machine learning. First, you have to be able to pick out the right algorithm, and there are quite a few different ones that you can pick from as you will see later on as we progress through this book. The algorithm that you end up picking out needs to have a good balance of things like accuracy, training time, complexity, and a number of parameters. And as you work more with machine learning, you will notice that each project will need a different combination of these factors. Using the probability theory and statistics, you can better pick out the right parameters for the program, the validation strategies, and make sure that you pick out the right algorithm for your needs. They can be helpful as well for letting you know what level of uncertainty is present inside of your choice so you can guess how much you can trust what is going on.

The probability theory and statistics will help you out quite a bit when it comes to working in machine learning and can help you to understand what is going on with the projects you are working on.

Looking at random variables

Now, the first topic we need to look at when it comes to statistics is random variables. With probability theory, these random variables will be expressed with the "X" symbol, and it is the variable that has all its possible variables come out as numerical outcomes that will come up during one of your random experiments. With random variables, there will be either continuous or discrete options. This means that sometimes your random variables will be functions that will map outcomes to the real value inside their space. We will look at a few examples of this one to help it make sense later on.

We will start out with an example of a random variable by throwing a die. The random variable that we will look at will be represented by X, and it will rely on the outcome that you will get once the die is thrown. The choices of X that would come naturally here will go through to map out the outcome denoted as 1 to the value of i.

What this means is that if X equals 1, you would map the event of throwing a one on your die to being the value of i. You would be able to map this out with any number that is on the die, and it is even possible to take it to the next step and pick out some mappings that are a bit strange. For example, you could map out Y to make it the outcome of 0. This can be a hard process to do, and we aren't going to spend much time on it, but it can help you to see how it works. When we are ready to write out his one, we would have the probability, which is shown as P of outcome 1 of random variable X. it would look like the following:

PX(i) or (x=i)

Distribution

Now we need to look at what the probability distribution is like with this process. What we mean here is that we will look at see what the probability of each outcome will be for the random variable. Or, to make it simple, we will see how likely it is that we will get a specific number, like a six or a three, when we throw the die.

To get started with this, we will need to look at an example. We will let the X, or the random variable, be our outcome that we get once the diet is thrown. We will also start with the assumption that the die is not loaded so that all six sides will have the same probability of showing up each time that you throw the diet. The probability distribution for throwing your die and getting a specific number includes:

$PX(1) = PX(2) = ... = PX(6) = 1/6$

In this example, it matches up to the what we did with the random variables, it does have a different type of meaning. Your probability distribution is more about the spectrum of events that can happen, while our random variable example is all about which variables are there. With the probability theory, the P(X) part will note that we are working with our probability distribution of the random variable X.

While looking through these examples, you can notice that your distribution will sometimes include two or more variables at the same time. When this happens, we will call it a joint distribution. Your probability will now be determined by each of the variables if there are more than one, that is now involved.

To see how this process will work, let's say that the X is random and that it is defined by what outcome you get when you throw the die, and the Y will be a random variable that will tell you what results that you get when you flip a coin. We will assign a 1 to this coin toss if we get heads at the end, and a 0 will show up if you get tails. This makes it easier when we figure out what the probability distribution is for both of these variables.

Independence

Another variable that you can work with when doing machine learning is to figure out how much independence the problem has. When you are doing random variables, you will find that they will end up being independent of what the other random variables are as long as the variable distribution doesn't change when a new variable is introduced to the equation.

You can make some assumptions about your data in machine learning to help make things easier when you already know about the independence. An example of this is the training sample of "j and i" will be independent of any underlying space when the label of sample "i" is unaffected by the features sample "j". No matter what one of the variables turns out, the other one is not going to be affected by that.

Think back to the example of the die and the coin flip. It doesn't matter what number shows up on the die. The coin will have its own result. And the same can be said the other way around as well. The X random variable is always going to be independent of the Y variable. It doesn't matter the value of Y, but the following code needs to be true for it:

$P(X) = P(X|Y)$.

In the case above, the values that come up for X and for Y variables are dropped because, at this point, the values of these variables are not going to matter that much. But with the statement above, it is true for any type of value that you provide to your X or Y, so it isn't going to matter what values are placed in this equation.

The Building Blocks Needed for Machine Learning

There are some algorithms that you will want to learn how to use to do well when you work on machine learning. But before we get to those, it is important to learn a few of the basic building blocks of machine learning. Doing this will really help you when you are ready to work with the machine learning algorithms.

These algorithms are great because they help you to do a lot of amazing things in machine learning, and they are the main reason why you would want to use machine learning.

The learning framework

Let's say that you decide that it is time to go on vacation to a new island. The natives that you meet on this island are really interested in eating papaya, but you have very limited experience with this kind of food. But you decide that it is good to give it a try and head on down to the marketplace, hoping to figure out which papaya is the best and will taste good to you.

Now, you have a few options as to how you would figure out which papaya is the best for you. You could start by asking some people at the marketplace which papayas are the best. But since everyone will have their own opinion about it, you will end up with lots of answers. You can also use some of your past experiences to do it.

At some point or another, you have worked with fresh fruit. You could use this to help you to make a good

222

choice. You may look at the color of the papaya and the softness to help you make a decision. As you look through the papaya, you will notice that there are a ton of colors, from dark browns to reds, and even different degrees of softness, so it is confusing to know what will work the best.

Learner's input

The first section of the framework that you need to look at is called the learner's input. To do this, you need to find a domain set and then focus on it. This domain can be an arbitrary set that is found in the objects, which in this framework is known as the points, that you need to get labeled. So, going back to the exercise about the papaya, you would have the domain set be any of the papayas that you are checking out. Then the domain points would be able to use the vectors of features, which in this case includes the softness and color of the fruit.

Once you have determined what domain points and domain sets you want to use, you can then go through and create the label set that you will use. In this exercise, the label set will hold onto the predictions that you will make about the papayas. You can look at each papaya and then make a prediction on how it tastes and whether it is the best one for you.

The label set that you get with this exercise will have two elements. The X will be any of the papayas that you think will taste bad. And then the Y will be the ones that you feel taste the best.

From here, you can work on what is known as the training data. This training data will be a set which can hold the sequence pairs that you will use when testing the accuracy of your predictions. So, with the exercise of the papayas, the training data will be the papayas that you decide to purchase. You will then take these home and taste them to see what tastes the best. This can help you to make better decisions later on when you purchase papayas. If you find that you really like a specific softness or color, ensure that you purchase that kind the next time.

Learner's output

Now that you have your input in, you will want to work on the output. The output is basically going to be the creation of a rule of prediction. It often goes by the name of predictor, classifier, or hypothesis, which you will then use to take the domain points and label them. With the papaya example, this rule will be the standard, which you get to set to where you want, and which will be used to help you figure out whether a papaya that you purchase will taste good or not, even before you eat it in the future.

When you first start, you are basically making guesses because you have no idea which papaya will be good or not. You can use some of your experiences from the past to help if you want, but since you haven't had a papaya before, it is hard to know what will taste good or not. But as you try out papayas and get some more experience with them, you will find that your future predictions will get much better.

Data generalization model

Once you have done the learner's input and output, you will need to take a look at what is known as a data generalization model. This model is nice because it can help you to create your own data for training based on the probability distribution of the domain sets that you used with the papayas. With this example, the model will be the method that you will use to decide what papayas you want to grab at the market to test them out at home.

In the beginning, you may not have any idea of what the distribution is. The data generalization model is designed to help you out, even if you don't know which ones to pick out from the beginning.

Measure of success

Before you can take time to work with the model above, you must make sure that you have some sort of method in place that can help you figure out whether you are successful or not in the project. There are a ton of options that you can choose with the papayas, but there must be some indicator along the way that will help you make the best predictions about whether you will see that success that you want or not.

Since the goal of this experiment is to help you figure out the fruits that will taste the best, so you are set in the future to get the ones that you like, you can use the error of the predictor simply by making sure that you pick out a range of different types of papayas when you are at the market. With all of this variety, it is easier to taste them at home and figure out which ones you like the most. Make sure to write down your observations as you eat each one. This will help you when you go back to the market because then you are more likely to pick out the fruits that you like the best.

PAC learning strategies

While we spent some time talking about how to set up a hypothesis and a training data set to get started with learning strategies in the above section, we still haven't spent time learning about PAC learning, There are two parameters that need to be found in this kind of learning including the accuracy parameter and the output classifier.

First, we need to look at the accuracy parameter. This is the parameter that will be used to determine how often the output classifier that you set up at the start will be able to make correct predictions. These predictions need to be set up to be based on information that you provide. You can also work with what is known as a confidence parameter. This parameter will measure how likely it is that your predictor can reach a certain level of accuracy. Accuracy can be important based on the type of project that you are working on so you should definitely look into this kind of learning if your project needs to maintain a high level of accuracy.

There are several ways that PAC can come in handy when you are doing a project. You may want to use it when you do training data to help see how accurate the model you have is. you may want to bring it into the learning when you feel that some uncertainties will come up and you want to ensure that your computer can handle them. Keep in mind that any time you work with the PAC learning model; it is always going to generate a few random training sets that you should watch out for.

Generalization models in machine learning

In machine learning, when you are considering what the idea of generalization is about, you are basically seeing that there are two components present and you will need to use both of them before you can get through all the data. The components that need to be present include the reliability assumption and revisiting the true error rate.

Any time that you can work with this, and you can meet the reliability assumption, you will be able to expect that the algorithm that you use in machine learning to get the results is pretty reliable for helping you know the distribution. But, there are also times when the assumption that you make here is not going to be very practical. This means that the standards that you picked out may have been unrealistic and that you went with the wrong algorithm to get all the work done.

In addition, the type of algorithm that you try to pick out for machine learning doesn't guarantee that you come up with a hypothesis that is something you like. Unlike using the Bayes predictor, which is an algorithm we will talk about more, later on, these algorithms are not set up to find which type of error rate is the best for you either.

In machine learning, there will be times when you need to make assumptions and use the experience that you have, either in that area or a similar area, to get things done. In some cases, you may even need to do some experimenting to figure out what you want to do. But machine learning can help to get this done.

These are the basic building blocks that you will need to understand and use when you are doing machine learning. These are so important because they can help you see how the programs that run on machine learning are working.

Conclusion

Thank you for making it to the end of this book. The impact of Machine Learning on our world is already ubiquitous. Our cars, our phones, our houses, and so much more are already being controlled and maintained through rudimentary Machine Learning systems. But in the future, Machine Learning will radically change the world. Some of those changes are easy to predict. In the next decade or two, people will no longer drive cars, instead, automated cars will drive people. But in many other ways, the effect of Machine Learning on our world is difficult to predict. Will Machine Learning algorithms replace so many jobs, from trucking to accounting, to many other disciplines, that there won't be much work left for people? In 100 years, will there be work for anyone at all? We don't know the answer to questions like this because there is so far no limit to what Machine Learning can accomplish, given time and data and the will to use it to achieve a particular task.

The future is not necessarily frightening. If there is no work in the future, it won't mean that things aren't getting done. Food will still be grown, picked, transported to market, and displayed in stores. It's just that people won't have to do any of that labor. As a matter of fact, stores won't be necessary either, since the food we order can be delivered directly to our homes. What will the world be like if human beings have almost unlimited leisure time? Is this a possible future?

There is no telling where this technology will take us in the future. Right now it is one of the most talked about topics in the field of IT. This is primarily because of its amazing potential in so many areas.

If technology continues to improve at such a rapid rate, there is a good chance that in the not too distant future, machines themselves will be programming other machines. At that point, the best question to ask is not what machines will be doing in the future but what will we?

This book provides information on what machine learning is and types of machine learning. It also gives you information on the subjects that laid the foundation for machine learning. You will gather information on different algorithms used in machine learning. As a beginner, it is always good to practice some algorithms used in machine learning to enhance your understanding. There are some projects in the book that you can complete over the weekend or extend them if you want to. It is important to practice as much as you can to improve your knowledge on machine learning. It is difficult to remember the many words that are used in machine learning.